Sanctify Them . . . That the World May Know

Sanctify Them . . . That the World May Know

Twelve Holiness Sermons

by
The General Superintendents
Church of the Nazarene
(1985-1989)

Nazarene Publishing House
Kansas City, Missouri

Contents

Foreword

It is incumbent upon every Nazarene minister, called of God, to preach the doctrine and experience of holiness of heart and life.

You will find in these 12 sermons written by the general superintendents of the Church of the Nazarene, biblical truths concerning "holiness without which no man shall see the Lord."

The need of preaching scriptural holiness from our pulpits is of paramount importance, especially in the context of our Wesleyan and Arminian persuasion.

It is our hope and prayer that these sermons will stir every heart and mind to the preaching of our cardinal doctrine.

M. A. "Bud" Lunn

Preface

Of vital concern to the Board of General Superintendents is the preservation and promulgation of the message we believe God has specially entrusted with the Church of the Nazarene, the glorious truth of Christian holiness.

The crowning work of the Holy Spirit, we believe, is entire sanctification or Christian perfection. It is our faith that through the gracious ministry of the Holy Spirit the Christian believer may be made pure in heart, perfect in love, and empowered for holy life and service. To proclaim this scriptural truth is the supreme privilege and primary responsibility of the Nazarene ministry.

In one sense every declaration of a Spirit-filled preacher, if he is true to his faith, is a declaration of Christian holiness, for this truth is at the very heart of biblical revelation. Many passages, however, bring to clear focus the call and promise of *full* salvation, as Dr. Bresee would say. These mountain peaks of holiness truth stand out in Holy Scripture and must be clearly and faithfully proclaimed so that our people will understand, seek, and find a pure heart and the fullness of the Holy Spirit.

Christian holiness is a doctrine to be believed, an experience to be received, and a life to be lived. The sermons in this volume reflect this view of the truth. They are submitted to our pastors and people with the conviction that they represent, in an imperfect form as we are the

9

first to admit, what the Spirit would say to the Church of the Nazarene at this juncture of our history.

We rejoice in the fresh urgency to evangelize, plant new churches, and penetrate new world areas as we move toward 1 million full members by 1995. But our very success could prove our undoing unless we remember Dr. Bresee's reminder, "We are debtors to every man to give him the gospel *in the same measure as we have received it*," the measure of *entire sanctification.* In order to remind us all afresh that we have been raised of God to "spread scriptural holiness to the ends of the earth," the Board of General Superintendents submits this volume of sermons.

WILLIAM M. GREATHOUSE
for the BOARD OF GENERAL SUPERINTENDENTS

Sanctify Them . . . That the World May Know

EUGENE L. STOWE

General Superintendent

Eugene L. Stowe was born in Council Bluffs, Iowa, in 1922. His parents were longtime members of Broadway Methodist Church in that city. This was the last pastorate served by Dr. P. F. Bresee before he moved to California in 1883 and later organized the First Church of the Nazarene in Los Angeles.

In 1938 the Stowe family moved to California and began to attend the Church of the Nazarene in Santa Monica. In 1939 Dr. Stowe was converted in revival services in that church and subsequently joined the church. He enrolled in Pasadena College that fall. During his sophomore year he felt a growing conviction that God was calling him to the preaching ministry. He made a total commitment of his life to Christ, which included answering that call, and received the sanctifying fullness of the Holy Spirit.

During his college years he met Miss Faye Cantrell, who was a student from Porterville, Calif. After a two-year courtship they were married in 1943. They have two sons, Don and Lynn, and a daughter, Gayla.

Since the denomination did not have a seminary at this time, he enrolled in the master of arts in religion program at the college, studying under Dr. H. Orton Wiley and Dr. Olive M. Winchester. Between 1944 and 1963 he and Mrs. Stowe served pastorates in California, Oregon, and Idaho, the last being a 10-year assignment at the College Church in Nampa. For 6 of these years he also taught in the Department of Religion at Northwest Nazarene College. In 1963 he was appointed to the superintendency of the new Central California District and subsequently served as president of Nazarene Theological Seminary. He was elected to the general superintendency in 1968.

DAVID'S PRAYER FOR FULL SALVATION

SCRIPTURE: Psalm 51:1-17

Introduction

The king had sinned a great sin. Tempted by the sight of a beautiful woman, he had allowed temptation to mate with his will, and lust was conceived. From there it was only a short step to sin. In hot blood he committed adultery, and then in cold blood he committed murder.

In this psalm David sets forth the way back to God. He lived centuries before Calvary and Pentecost. He knew nothing about justification and sanctification. But by divine revelation he gives us the clear steps to full salvation.

Step 1. *The Frank Acknowledgment of Sin in Penitence and Confession*

Listen again to the words of verse 3: "I know my transgressions, and my sin is always before me" (NIV).* There is no rationalization; no blaming a wife who was incompatible. He accepted the indictment of Isa. 59:2: "Your iniquities have separated you from your God; your sins have hidden his face from you." There is no cover-up. With the wise man he faced the fact that "he that covereth his sins shall not prosper" (Prov. 28:13, KJV).

---

*Unless otherwise indicated, all Scripture quotations in this chapter are from *The Holy Bible, New International Version.*

13

Furthermore, he was willing to humble himself before God. Though this was a public sin, as king he was not accountable to his subjects. There was no human authority by which he could be judged or punished. But he acknowledged that he was accountable to God who could judge and punish him. "Have mercy on me, O God . . . Against you, you only, have I sinned and done what is evil in your sight" (vv. 1, 4). And the king prostrates himself before the King of Kings in a spirit of utter contrition. In verses 16 and 17 he acknowledges that not animal sacrifices but "a broken spirit: a broken and contrite heart" are the only offerings that are appropriate for him to bring to God. The Hebrew word used here literally means to break into pieces, to completely shatter. David was a broken man; he had gone all the way down.

Then it is important for us to notice that David acknowledges the twofold nature of his sin. In verse 3 he speaks of his committed sins: "I know my transgressions, and my sin is always before me." But he goes on to admit that his acts of sin stemmed from original sin. Listen to verse 5: "Surely I was sinful at birth, sinful from the time my mother conceived me." His sinful nature had been inherited from his parents, and they in turn had inherited their depravity from their foreparents all the way back to Adam.

This is still where salvation begins. One's sin must be acknowledged—no rationalizing, no excusing, no covering up. Like the publican of old, our cry must be "God be mericful to me a sinner" (Luke 18:13, KJV). Then in an attitude of true humility and brokenness, there must be genuine repentance. To repent means literally to change one's mind about sin. Instead of accepting it, there must

14

be total rejection. Instead of loving it, there must be a holy hatred for it. Such godly sorrow for sin will naturally lead to a prayer of full confession such as King David prayed.

This is the picture of the criminal who throws himself upon the mercy of the court. Condemned by his own conscience, he does not wait to be convicted and arrested. Rather, he goes to the legal authorities and confesses his wrongdoing.

Step 2. *By Faith Accept the Forgiveness and Cleansing Promised by God*

The foundation for David's faith is found in the very first verse: "Have mercy on me, O God, according to your unfailing love; according to your great compassion." Isaiah echoes this same sublime certainty in the 55th chapter of his prophecy, verses 6 and 7: "Seek the Lord while he may be found; call on him while he is near. Let the wicked forsake his way and the evil man his thoughts. Let him turn to the Lord, and he will have mercy on him, and to our God, for he will freely pardon." With this divine assurance he could believe that God would blot out his transgressions.

This is totally different from the prospect faced by the confessed criminal in the courts of our country. The judge is under no compulsion to show mercy. He may demand the full penalty of the law. But David knew the character of his Judge. "Unfailing love" and "great compassion" are the attributes of His character. On this basis he could believe that God would "blot out [his] transgressions." Here the Psalmist resorts to language of the courts. A legal indictment was written against every

15

criminal. However, if the judge showed mercy and forgiveness, a fluid was applied to the parchment that completely erased the printing of the indictment. It was totally blotted out. There were no charges against the criminal.

What a picture this is of the glorious truth of justification. Through the grace of God the forgiven sinner is completely justified—just-as-if-he had never sinned. What a miracle! Sins forgiven and forgotten. No charges against me. I am completely free from guilt and condemnation.

Songwriter Merrill Dunlop expresses it in these beautiful words:

> *What a wondrous message in God's Word!*
> *My sins are blotted out, I know!*
> *If I trust in His redeeming blood,*
> *My sins are blotted out, I know!**

Great as this is, there is more. Just as sin is twofold, so is salvation. John Wesley placed strong emphasis upon the fact that the Scriptures taught that full salvation consists of both justification and sanctification. The word "sanctification" means to be made holy. This process begins at justification. At the same time one is justified he is also regenerated or born of the Holy Spirit. This brings about a real as well as a relational change in one's life. The very fact that the Spirit of God is revealed as the *Holy* Spirit means that when He comes to dwell in the heart He brings the holiness of God. For Mr. Wesley, justification initiates sanctification. What a glorious transformation! Paul described it by saying, "If anyone is in Christ, he is a new creation; the old has gone, the new has come!" (2 Cor. 5:17).

It is easy for the newly converted to imagine that all sin is gone. But it is seldom long before one finds that original sin was only suspended, not destroyed—stunned, but not dead. There are now two principles within—one is the new nature, and the other is the old. With Paul they raise this agonizing question, "Who will rescue me from this body of death?" (Rom. 7:24).

The Psalmist realized this when he prayed in verse 2, "Wash away all my iniquity and cleanse me from my sin." His sins had been forgiven, but the old nature of sin that he had inherited was still present. He goes on with his prayer in verse 7: "Cleanse me with hyssop, and I will be clean; wash me, and I will be whiter than snow." He cries out for full salvation in verse 10 when he supplicates, "Create in me a clean heart, O God; and renew a right spirit within me."

Bible scholars tell us that the Hebrew language in which the Old Testament was written has two words for washing. The first is the one that is applied to the washing of the body or kitchen utensils—anything that can be dipped in water or have water poured over it. This is a superficial, surface cleansing. However, the second word is a very special term that is used to describe the washing of garments by beating them with a stick or pounding them on a rock submerged in water. Many times in our foreign travel Mrs. Stowe and I have seen women washing their clothes in a stream. To get out the ground-in dirt they must rub and scrub the garments unmercifully on rocks. Only then will the clothes be really clean. The

17

Psalmist deliberately chooses this second word. What a picture this is of the purifying of the heart from inbred, inherited sin. This is much more than luxuriating in a warm shower with mild bath soap. The nature of sin is so entrenched in human nature that only the deep cleansing provided by the blood of Jesus Christ through the agency of the powerful Holy Spirit can destroy it.

This is what happened on the Day of Pentecost. The disciples were believers. They had accepted Christ as Messiah and Savior. But the nature of sin had not been cleansed. Jesus commanded them to wait in the Upper Room for the baptism with the Holy Spirit. Acts 2:4 records that on the Day of Pentecost they were all filled with the Holy Spirit. He not only empowered them for witnessing when He came, but He also cleansed them from inbred sin. Their lives were different. Self-will was crucified with Christ, and now they sought only to do His will. This inner purity would be lived out in lives of loving service.

The sanctifying, cleansing baptism with the Holy Spirit is still God's will for every believer. Jesus promised, "Blessed are those who hunger and thirst for righteousness, for they will be filled" (Matt. 5:6). But this filling comes only to those who have a consuming desire for righteousness. William Barclay tells us that the words of Jesus are not in the genitive case, which means to casually drink some water or eat some food. Rather, they are in the accusative case—this is total hunger and thirst. The songwriter expressed it in these words:

Lord Jesus, I long to be perfectly whole;
I want Thee forever to live in my soul.

18

Break down ev'ry idol, cast out ev'ry foe.
Now wash me and I shall be whiter than snow.
—JAMES NICHOLSON

Conclusion

My friend, are you longing for the full salvation? Pray David's prayer of confession and find forgiveness for your sin. Perhaps you have been saved but have not found full deliverance from the nature of sin. Give your whole self to God. Let the blood of Jesus Christ, God's Son, cleanse you from all sin. God has promised to "sanctify you through and through" (1 Thess. 5:23). Let Him do it now.

PERFECT, PRESENT CLEANSING

Introduction

One of the great old gospel songs that our people have always sung with great gusto is "Standing on the Promises." Almost without exception the songleader will make one of two comments as he introduces the song:

1. "Let's stand as we sing, because it's almost impossible to stand on the promises sitting down"; or

2. "What we need around this church is for more of our people to quit sitting on the premises and start standing on the promises."

Then invariably he will say, "We will sing stanzas 1, 2, and 4."

What a tragedy to miss the blessed assurance of these words in stanza 3:

Standing on the promises I now can see
Perfect, present cleansing in the Blood for me.

Whether our Calvinist friends believe it or not, and whether some of our Arminian people experience it or not, the fact remains—there is "perfect, present cleansing in the Blood for me"! Not because a songwriter named Kelso Carter wrote these words almost a century ago, but because this glorious provision stands upon the rock-solid promises made by Almighty God thousands of years ago.

Scripture Text

Six hundred years before Christ's birth, the prophet Ezekiel issued a tremendous proclamation through the inspiration of the Holy Spirit. It is contained in Ezek. 36:25-27 (NIV).* While this assurance is directed immediately to the house of Israel, it is for us all today.

"I will sprinkle clean water on you, and you will be clean; I will cleanse you from all your impurities and from all your idols. I will give you a new heart and put a new spirit in you; I will remove from you your heart of stone and give you a heart of flesh. And I will put my Spirit in you and move you to follow my decrees and be careful to keep my laws."

This glorious promise formed one of the scriptural cornerstones in John Wesley's doctrine of Christian per-

---

*Unless otherwise indicated, all Scripture quotations in this chapter are from *The Holy Bible, New International Version.*

fection. The explicit language of the text clearly speaks of cleansing that is both perfect and present.

I. *From the Beginning the Holiness of God Has Made Perfect Cleansing for His Children an Absolute Necessity*

The word "holiness" and its derivatives appear 617 times in the Bible. "Purity" and its kindred words are found more than 450 times in the Scriptures. As early as the Exodus from Egypt the Word of the Lord commanded, "You are to be my holy people" (Exod. 22:31). His chosen ones were to be separated from the heathen idolatries and other sinful practices of the pagan people with whom they would be associated. But not only were they to be separated *from* the unholiness around them, they were to be separated *to* their holy God.

The following book, Leviticus, makes it clear that like Father, like sons: "Consecrate yourselves and be holy, because I am holy" (11:44). Reading on in this book of laws and in the Book of Numbers, we find the prescriptions for all kinds of ceremonial cleansings and purification rites. Very specific instructions are given to priests as to the personal cleanliness that was required before they entered the holy place in their immaculate sacerdotal garments. All the gory details of the required animal sacrifices for the sin offerings are outlined explicitly.

But from our vantage point we can clearly see that these ceremonies were more ritual than real. After all these elaborate formalities had been conducted, cleansing was both imperfect and impermanent. It was all on the outside. God's people were really no different on the in-

21

side. This became painfully evident as their impure hearts repeatedly led them off into idol worship and other sinful practices.

A century before Ezekiel penned these words, Isaiah had confronted his own personal impurity when he worshiped in the Temple. He heard the seraphic choir sing, "Holy, holy, holy is the Lord Almighty." His response was, "Woe to me! . . . I am ruined! For I am a man of unclean lips" (Isa. 6:3, 5).

All this is ancient history. Has God changed His mind about the absolute necessity of personal purity? First Pet. 1:15-16 repeats this timeless demand for holiness: "But just as he who called you is holy, so be holy in all you do; for it is written: 'Be holy, because I am holy.'" The requirement has not lessened. Modern man is not excused from this mandate.

Preaching before the British Parliament in the year 1647, Ralph Cudworth, professor of Hebrew at Cambridge University, stated the case in these words: "The end of the gospel is not merely to cover sinne by spreading the Purple Robe of Christ's death and suffering over it, whilst it still remaineth in us with all its filth and noisomness unremoved; but also to convey a powerful and mighty spirit of holinesse, to cleanse us and free us from it." More recently, Dr. John A. Redhead, eminent Southern Presbyterian pastor, continually stresses from both pulpit and pen that a morally holy God demands moral holiness in His people.

This truth needs constant reemphasis in light of the contemporary teaching of some evangelicals that cleansing is only partial and holiness incomplete. They have reasoned that the blood of Christ covers the sins of the

Christian like a white blanket of snow covers the filth of the farmyard. But Dr. W. T. Purkiser has wisely observed that this sounds good, but what happens when the spring thaw comes? Thank God for the promise of Ezek. 36:25, "I will cleanse you from *all* your impurities and from *all* your idols" (italics added). John employs this extravagant wording when he assures us that "if we walk in the light, as he is in the light, we have fellowship one with another, and the blood of Jesus Christ his Son cleanseth us from all sin" (1 John 1:7, KJV).

Yes, God's requirement is still that His children shall be conformed to His holy image by virtue of the perfect cleansing that He has provided through His Son, our Sanctifier.

II. *Furthermore, God's Word Guarantees That This Perfect Cleansing Is a Present Possibility*

From the pinnacle of divine revelation, the prophet caught a glimpse of the great salvation that God was going to provide. This would come about through the agency of the Second Person of the Trinity, Jesus Christ, and the Third Person, the Holy Spirit.

It all begins with a "new heart" that replaces the "heart of stone" that has been removed (Ezek. 36:26). That stony, sinful heart motivated Israel to rebel and disobey time after time as God tried to lead them from captivity to Canaan. And hearts of stone in modern-day rebels can only be softened and made obedient to the Lord when the Great Physician performs a spiritual heart transplant operation. Paul prays in Eph. 3:17 "that Christ may dwell in your hearts through faith." When one confesses his sins and opens the door of his heart to the Savior, His promise is, "I will come in" (Rev. 3:20). This is the miracle of regeneration. "If anyone is in Christ, he is a new creation; the old has gone, the new has come!" (2 Cor. 5:17).

Oswald Chambers points out that this is more than erasing the record of the past: "Forgiveness means not merely that a man is saved from sin . . . forgiveness means that I am saved from sinning."[1] The new heart activates the mind to think pure thoughts and motivates the will to make the right moral decisions. Yes, cleansing begins at conversion.

But cleansing is not completed in the new birth. Sins are forgiven, but the inherited nature of sin is still present in the heart. Perfect cleansing must destroy this original sin as well. Both Roman Catholics and Protestants agree at this point.

The question of consequence is, "When does total cleansing take place?" Catholics teach that original sin is burned out in the fire of purgatory after death. Many Protestants believe that in "the hour and article of death" one receives a clean heart. In this regard, Clovis Chappell states, "Death has no power to change character. If the mere act of dying could make a bad man good, then that same experience might make a good man bad. I am sure that the quality of life will be the same after death as it was before."[2]

This passage in Ezekiel assures us that we do not have to wait this long. Cleansing is not postmortem. After the promise of the new heart and new spirit, God's promise is "I will . . . move you to follow my decrees and be careful to keep my laws" (v. 27). There will be no decrees or laws in heaven. Therefore, the inescapable conclusion is that heart purity may be received in this life. *It is a present possibility!*

In the 18th century, John Wesley became convinced on the basis of this passage in Ezekiel and other similar scriptures that there was a "second blessing, rightly so called" that completed the cleansing begun in regeneration. Justification, or initial sanctification, provided the remedy for actual sin and entire sanctification accomplished the purifying of the heart from original sin. In his classic treatise, *A Plain Account of Christian Perfection,* he declared, "We do not know a single instance, in any place, of a person's receiving, in one and the same moment, remission of sins, the abiding witness of the Spirit, and a new, a clean heart."[3] He insisted that "salvation . . . begins the moment we are justified, . . . in another instant, the heart is cleansed from all sin."[4] This instantaneous work of entire sanctification would be followed by growth in grace and holy living, said Wesley.

An increasing number of voices outside of our Wesleyan circles are acknowledging this truth. Dr. Alan Redpath puts it in these words:

> None can ever ascend unto the hill of the Lord except he has clean hands and a pure heart, for without holiness no man can see the Lord. And if we are going to stand before Him with clean hands and a pure heart . . . our lives [will have to be] made pure by the blood of Jesus Christ. . . . Nobody can know what the victorious life is merely by going to Calvary to be forgiven; he must stay at Calvary . . . until he knows something of what it means for the Holy Spirit to crucify his lust, and his affections, and his desires.[5]

On the Day of Pentecost, God kept His promise made in Ezek. 36:27—"I will put my Spirit in you." One hundred twenty believers were baptized with the cleansing, empowering fullness of the Holy Spirit. Their carnal self-will was put to death, and they became totally devoted to finding and doing God's will. In Acts 15:9, Peter testifies to the purifying of the believers' hearts in the Upper Room, as well as at the house of Cornelius.

Since that time, millions have borne witness to a second work of grace in their lives. One of the great evangelical leaders of our time, the late Dr. Harold John Ockenga, tells of his own experience in these words, "I was a Christian for some years, was preaching the gospel, was experiencing fruit in my ministry before I felt the deep need and the compelling necessity of waiting to be filled with the Holy Spirit. Once this happened . . . the entire quality of my spiritual experience was changed." He continues, "He sanctifies the individual creating a holy life by renewing the entire disposition."[6]

And this biblical blessing is for all believers today. The blood of Jesus Christ is the procuring cause of entire sanctification. The Holy Spirit is its efficient cause. The provision has been made. Believers may now receive this glorious gift of the Father.

Dr. John Seamands of Asbury Seminary lists these four essential steps that will lead one into the experience of full salvation:

1. *Recognize your inner impurity and conflict. . . .*
2. *Have faith to believe that the Holy Spirit is able to reach down and work in depths that are beyond your control. . . .*
3. *Pray a definite prayer to the Holy Spirit for your personal cleansing. . . .*

26

4. *Maintain an attitude of surrender and obedience.*[7]

This cleansing crisis initiates the process of continuous cleansing as our wills remain surrendered and we
keep on walking in the light. We practice this principle
every time we drive our cars at night. The illumination
from the headlights only pierces the darkness for a dis-
tance of 200 feet. But that is sufficient, for as we travel
forward in that light we continue to see far enough ahead
to make safe progress in our journey.

Praise God for perfect, present cleansing that is able
to "preserve [us] blameless unto the coming of our Lord
Jesus Christ" (1 Thess. 5:23, KJV).

CHARLES H. STRICKLAND

General Superintendent

Dr. Charles H. Strickland was converted in 1924 and sanctified in the revival that started the Church of the Nazarene in Waycross, Ga., in 1928. He became a charter member of that church. After attending Trevecca Nazarene College, he began his pastoral ministry in 1937, serving three Georgia churches: Moultrie, Waycross, and Atlanta. After 2 years as Florida district superintendent and 2 years in the pastorate of Dallas First Church, he moved, in 1948, to South Africa. For 17 years he was district superintendent of the European work in that area. During this time he helped develop the Nazarene Bible College in South Africa, serving as president for 1 year.

In 1965 Dr. Strickland returned to the States to oversee plans for the Nazarene Bible College in Colorado Springs. In 1967 he became the first president for the school and remained in this position until 1972 when the Eighteenth General Assembly elected him to the Board of General Superintendents.

Dr. Strickland is married to the former Fanny K. McManus. They have four sons: Rev. Charles E. Strickland, Santa Rosa, Calif.; Mr. Robert Wayne Strickland, Colorado Springs, Colo.; Dr. Dudley K. Strickland, Olney, Md.; and Mr. Douglas K. Strickland, Oklahoma City.

THE CALL TO HOLINESS

SCRIPTURE: 1 Peter 1:15-16

"But as he which hath called you is holy, so be ye holy in all manner of conversation; because it is written, Be ye holy; for I am holy."

Our beloved church as we know it today is the result of a great doctrinal heritage created through the revival spirit of the latter part of the 19th century. At this time the great Wesleyan doctrine of sanctification and the life of holiness as taught in the Scriptures became the major theme of the revival, and from this the Church of the Nazarene has its historic roots.

This great doctrine is enunciated so clearly in the words of our text: "Be ye holy; for I am holy." This is God's order; this is God's command. Let us examine it and its implications in personal experience.

The text declares that God desires a holy people. We hear this theme in the Old Testament. In Lev. 11:45 we read: "For I am the Lord that bringeth you up out of the land of Egypt, to be your God: ye shall therefore be holy, for I am holy." We hear it again in the beautiful words of Ezek. 36:25-26: "Then will I sprinkle clean water upon you, and ye shall be clean: from all your filthiness, and from all your idols, will I cleanse you. A new heart also will I give you, and a new spirit will I put within you: and I will take away the stony heart out of your flesh, and I will give you an heart of flesh." We hear it once again in Ps. 24:3-4: "Who shall ascend into the hill of the Lord? or who shall stand in his holy place? He that hath clean hands, and a pure heart."

This is the message also of the New Testament. Zacharias the priest, on the occasion of the birth of his son John the Baptist, declared, "That we being delivered out of the hand of our enemies might serve him without fear, in holiness and righteousness before him, all the days of our life" (Luke 1:74-75). In His great Sermon on the Mount, Jesus commanded, "Be ye therefore perfect, even as your Father which is in heaven is perfect" (Matt. 5:48). We hear this cry again in 2 Cor. 7:1 as Paul admonishes the Corinthian church: "Having therefore these promises, dearly beloved, let us cleanse ourselves from all filthiness of the flesh and spirit, perfecting holiness in the fear of God." It is God's desire that people be holy. God wants us to be like Him. It is natural that a human father desires his child to become a likeness of himself. God also desires likeness in His creation. He has willed that we should be holy. He has provided this possibility that we may be.

We draw from human experience as we look again at this text. People need this provision of holiness that God has made possible for them. Man must have God's continuous and enabling power. Three reasons make this fact very evident.

1. *People need God's holiness to restore their communion with God*

Communion with God was broken. Man sinned against God. The Bible speaks truthfully when it says, "For all have sinned, and come short of the glory of God" (Rom. 3:23). It is a text of importance, for it declares the universal state of sin in every person born in the world. David says in Ps. 51:5, "In sin did my mother conceive me." Isaiah voices this sad condition in the 53rd chapter and verse 6: "All we like sheep have gone astray; we have turned every one to his own way." He voices eternal hope also by saying further, "The Lord hath laid on him [Christ] the iniquity of us all."

To restore this communion completely God must do two things for us. He must forgive the sins of the past and must also change the inner nature of a person to conform to His perfect will in the life of holiness. Two divine works of grace are necessary to complete this work of full salvation in our hearts. Sin is twofold: It is acts of disobedience that became action; it is also a spirit of disobedience that is the deep root of sin in the nature of man. The spirit of disobedience within becomes responsible for the acts of disobedience that become action sins. Both must be dealt with. Acts of sin must be forgiven. The inner spirit of disobedience must be cleansed. An act cannot be cleansed; it must be forgiven. A spirit or nature within the heart cannot be forgiven; it must be cleansed. Therefore to restore communion God has provided both forgiveness and cleansing in the great miracle of full salvation.

Examples of these two works of grace are abundant in the New Testament. We have several instances in the

31

Book of Acts itself that are given in connection with the evangelism of the New Testament Church. In Acts 8:5-17, Philip went to Samaria and preached Christ to the people, resulting in the Samaritan revival. There was great joy among the people who received the good news of the gospel. Later, Peter and John went to Samaria, and the Bible records in verse 15, "Who, when they were come down, prayed for them, that they might receive the Holy Ghost."

Again in Acts 9 Saul was traveling to Damascus with letters of authority to persecute the Church. En route he met with Jesus in a confrontation that resulted in his conversion. Instead of proceeding to Damascus to persecute the Christians, he humbly asked, "Lord, what wilt thou have me to do?" (v. 6). After his arrival, and following three days of fasting, God sent Ananias to him, who prayed for Saul to "receive thy sight, and be filled with the Holy Ghost" (v. 17).

Peter's experience with Cornelius in Acts 10 is also significant. Cornelius is described as "a devout man, and one that feared God with all his house, which gave much alms to the people, and prayed to God alway" (v. 2). He sent for Peter, the apostle. When Peter finally consented to visit him and preached to him and those assembled in his house, verse 44 records that "while Peter yet spake these words, the Holy Ghost fell on all them which heard the word."

We see this again in the Ephesian disciples when Paul asks them the question recorded in Acts 19:2, "Have ye received the Holy Ghost since ye believed? And they said unto him, We have not so much as heard whether there be any Holy Ghost." This is the message we have been trying to tell the world. We need the Holy Spirit to restore our communion with God.

2. *Man also needs holiness to maintain right relationships to his fellowmen*

All of us need a power beyond ourselves to maintain a correct relationship to our fellow human beings in today's complicated world. This was so evident in the life of the disciples. In Luke 9 we discover some great weaknesses among the disciples in their pre-Pentecost relationships. They were Christ's disciples; they were converted; they were commissioned to help Christ save the world; they were the foundation of the New Testament Church that was to be launched on the Day of Pentecost. In verse 46 we read: "There arose a reasoning among them, which of them should be greatest." Here is an example of person versus person. Each, no doubt, voted for himself. It is the common feeling that the human ego brings out in all of us the feeling of self-importance. It becomes a part of modern training to live and survive in a competitive world. But it does not fit the pattern of true discipleship.

We see another weakness exposed in the same chapter in verse 49: "Master, we saw one casting out devils in thy name; and we forbad him, because he followeth not with us." Here is an example of group versus group and represents a narrow sectarianism that has brought great division in the Christian Church. Jesus reminded the disciples that those who were not scattering from them were

33

for them. But the relationship problem goes to a higher level. The disciples were passing through Samaria. Relationships with the Samaritans were not good. Because the Samaritans did not prepare for them, we read in verse 54, "Lord, wilt thou that we command fire to come down from heaven, and consume them . . . ?" Here is the sorry specter of race against race that has brought so many great social problems into our human society.

Man needs the cleansing work of the Holy Spirit to maintain his ethical relationship toward his fellowman individually, in groups, and on a racial basis. The answer of the Master was, "Tarry ye in the city of Jerusalem, until ye be endued with power from on high" (Luke 24:49). One of the miracles of Pentecost recorded in Acts 2 was that on that great day they were "all with one accord in one place" (v. 1). Then came the blessed Holy Spirit.

3. *Man needs the Holy Spirit to maintain his own spiritual victory*

Modern persons cannot maintain a high spiritual level in their own strength. We have many precious people who have received Christ's forgiving grace and who have started forth in the Christian life. They are experiencing difficulty because of inner conflicts brought about by anger, jealousy, pride, and so on, which is described so adequately in Romans 7. We are not responsible for this condition, but how thankful we can be that full salvation

34

means we can be rid of it. "God hath not called us unto uncleanness, but unto holiness" (1 Thess. 4:7).

The text strongly implies that God has made provision for man's moral holiness. We hear it in the prayer of Jesus in John 17:17, "Sanctify [purify, Amp.] them through thy truth: thy word is truth." We hear it also in the description of the Atonement. In John 3:16 we hear God's great love announcement: "For God so loved the world, that he gave his only begotten Son, that whosoever believeth in him should not perish, but have everlasting life." Paul declares that "Christ also loved the church, and gave himself for it; that he might sanctify and cleanse it with the washing of water by the word, that he might present it to himself a glorious church, not having spot, or wrinkle, or any such thing; but that it should be holy and without blemish" (Eph. 5:25-27). It can be a personal experience according to Paul in 1 Thess. 5:23, "And the very God of peace sanctify you wholly; and I pray God your whole spirit and soul and body be preserved blameless unto the coming of our Lord Jesus Christ."

The prophet Isaiah in former chapters delivered a scathing pronouncement of judgment to Israel for their sins and opened the door of hope in chapter 35 in his beautiful description of God's restoration from the desert. He declares a great highway that will be built in the desert in verse 8: "And an highway shall be there, and a way, and it shall be called The way of holiness." In verse 10 he promises to those who walk on that highway that "the ransomed of the Lord shall return, and come to Zion with songs and everlasting joy upon their heads: they shall obtain joy and gladness, and sorrow and sighing shall flee away."

THE BEAUTY OF HOLINESS

SCRIPTURE: Luke 1:73-75

"The oath which he sware to our father Abraham, that he would grant unto us, that we being delivered out of the hand of our enemies might serve him without fear, in holiness and righteousness before him, all the days of our life."

The occasion was the birth and name announcement of John the Baptist. His father, Zacharias, was a devout priest in the Temple. An angel visited him in the course of his duties to tell him that a son would be born to him, despite the fact that his wife was beyond the normal age of childbearing. Moreover, this son would be a special messenger from the Lord to prepare the way of the coming of Jesus Christ. Following the announcement of the name of his son, Zacharias utters a prophetic statement on the coming of Jesus and gives us one of the clearest pronouncements concerning the mission and purpose of the coming of Christ and the complete adequacy of His atonement to restore the people to full communion with God.

This statement was taken to have a national meaning for the restoration of the Jewish nation of Israel and a deliverance from the Roman bondage under which they were oppressed at this time. The reference, however, to the oath given to Abraham long ago gives the passage a spiritual application. Abraham had offered his only son, Isaac, upon the altar of sacrifice in obedience to God's command. This tense drama is recorded in Genesis 22. At the last moment God provided a substitute sacrifice and then gave the oath to Abraham: "Because thou hast done this thing, and hast not withheld thy son, thine only son: that in blessing I will bless thee, and in multiplying I will multiply thy seed as the stars of the heaven, and as the sand which is upon the sea shore; and thy seed shall possess the gate of his enemies; and in thy seed shall all the nations of the earth be blessed; because thou hast obeyed my voice" (vv. 16-18).

The application of this promise applied to Christ's atoning work must be a spiritual fulfillment. Israel remained under bondage to Rome for a long period after the time of Christ, but spiritual freedom was given to both Jews and Gentiles on the Cross. Jesus really came to free man from the great enemy of sin and the spiritual slavery in which he found himself and to restore the human family to holiness that Adam lost in Eden. It was never God's plan for His people to live in spiritual bondage. God designed that man should serve Him in holiness, and Jesus came to restore that relationship.

It is evident that God's original design for His world as well as His people was a design that involved beauty and harmony. This is clearly evident in nature as well as in His relationships with His people. As we travel in and through our own country we do see evidence of God's design and beauty everywhere. The beautiful seashore with its rolling waves, its gorgeous sunsets, the mornings filled with the rising sun; the majestic mountains—lonely sentinels to the past; the great forests; the rich plains that became the breadbasket of the nation; the large pasturelands where cattle thrive—all bear testimony to beauty and design. The more we understand of our universe and the space that is around us we are reminded again of the beauty and design of a great Creator.

Holiness in character is God's greatest achievement. Jesus has paid for our complete restoration, and the door is now open to "serve him without fear, in holiness and righteousness before him, all the days of our life." As we examine the results of this provision in human experience, its beauty unfolds like the petals of a beautiful flower.

Holiness is beautiful first of all in its *purity:* "That we being delivered out of the hand of our enemies might serve him without fear." The greatest enemy of mankind is sin. In its essence sin is disobedience to God, a rebellion against His law, and actions against His will. This is given so clearly in our church constitution and is supported by the Holy Scriptures. Paragraph 5 of the 1985 *Manual* states: "We believe that sin came into the world through the disobedience of our first parents, and death by sin. We believe that sin is of two kinds: original sin or depravity, and actual or personal sin."[1] Genesis chapter 3 tells the sad story of man's fall into sin and his failure. In David's prayer that followed his shameful sin of adultery as well as murder we hear the tragic admission of original sin: "Behold, I was shapen in iniquity; and in sin did my mother conceive me" (Ps. 51:5). His plea in verse 10 is the universal cry of all humanity: "Create in me a clean heart, O God; and renew a right spirit within me."

The mission of Christ was to provide a once-and-for-all atonement for sin—both in act and in nature—giving the people of the world a deliverance from sin. This deliverance involves both a forgiveness of actual sins and a cleansing of the sinful nature that is the root cause of action sins. Both are necessary to complete one's total redemption and to bring us into a complete acceptance with God. It must be noted that we are not responsible for having a carnal nature. We were born with it. It becomes the root cause of human fear, anger, envy, jealousy, hate, and all like emotions that are basic in a person's nature. It is also not possible to have complete control over them by one's own efforts. The refinements of education may help some, but no person can completely control these basic emotions without help from God.

The great John Wesley came to America as a missionary to the Indians. En route from his native England the ship on which he was traveling encountered a storm on the high seas that threatened the lives of all on board. It was his great fear of death together with his own lack of assurance that made him become interested in a group of religious people on board who seemed to be without fear and who sang hymns during the storm. He learned much from these humble Moravians. Later he returned to England a failure, having found his formal training no match for the American frontier. Then he attended the Moravian meetings and encountered his great heart-warming experience at Aldersgate. This began his search for holiness and brought about the great Wesleyan revival in England and later in America.

This is a blessed deliverance from sin in both of its forms—actual and original. It is the message of the New Testament. It is the experience of thousands of God's people enabling them to "serve him without fear." I traveled for many years through South and Central Africa before the highways were paved. Traveling through Zambia on a very dusty highway, I observed one day a bush beside the road that had not become the dusty brown color of all the other plants and trees along the route. I examined its large leaves with a magnifying glass. This particular bush is necessary to the life of the jungle, so its leaves must not become clogged with dust. Nature provided it with a substance that rejects the dirt and dust, and I found that its leaves were totally free from dust. My observation that day beside the Zambian highway was that if God could keep a bush free from dirt in a world so dirty from the traffic on the highway, He could keep a person's life in a dirty world free from the filth of sinful living. Holiness is, therefore, beautiful in its purity.

Holiness is also beautiful in its *ability to lift the levels of human behavior* to "serve him . . . in holiness and righteousness before him." The terms "holiness and righteousness" are twins. Holiness refers to our relationship to God; righteousness refers to our relationship to our fellow-men. These are interdependent relationships. When we receive the gracious infilling with the Holy Spirit our hearts are made pure and holy toward God. This results in a higher level of behavioral patterns toward our fellowmen.

We are faced with a triangle of relationships in our daily existence. We have a relationship to God, we have a relationship to our fellowmen, and we establish a relationship to ourselves. Inner peace can be found only as these relationships are corrected and we learn to live in harmony in each relationship.

The experience of holiness places us in a right relationship with God. The Psalmist declares this in Ps. 24: 3-4, "Who shall ascend into the hill of the Lord? or who shall stand in his holy place?" And the answer is, "He that hath clean hands, and a pure heart."

When this basic relationship is established, the levels of behavior toward our fellowmen are lifted to enable us to obey the command: "Love thy neighbour as thyself." This is another key to inner peace. One cannot achieve any measure of inner tranquility and maintain a hate for another human being. Hate destroys the person who harbors it in his heart and is more detrimental to that person than to the object of his hatred. Dr. George Washington Carver, the famous Southern Black scientist, made a very famous remark: "I will never allow any man to bring me so low as to make me hate him." It is indeed beautiful to see "righteousness in action" in the development of good, solid relationships among the people of God. It operates so beautifully in our home relationships. Our social relationships, in our business relationships and in labor-manage-

41

ment situations, could be the groundwork of a happy national and international relationship. The principles of applied Christianity could prevent war and strife among the nations of the world.

The beauty of holiness is observed thirdly in its *permanence*. "All the days of our life." It is not, as some have tried to establish, merely an emotional state based upon a decision made in a revival meeting or a decision day at the church. It becomes a permanent life-style of the Christian and a growth pattern into which one grows daily in developing the beautiful fruit of the Spirit as described in Galatians 5. The consecrated Christian grows each day more into the likeness of Christ.

When I was a youth my parents lived for a while on a farm in the peach-growing section of Georgia. On our farm, of course, were large numbers of peach trees that produced the beautiful and large Alberta peaches. I can remember my mother, when the peach harvest was in, spending many hours canning and preserving the big Albertas. Her definition of the process was very simple. She would cook the peaches at just the right temperature with the correct amount of sweetening and then seal them in jars to prevent outside air from contacting the fruit. She was so sure of her success in this process that I heard her say many times, "I can keep them preserved sweet forever." We stored them in the basement of our home. Later when the snow was on the ground and the trees were bare, we enjoyed the delicious preserves.

The spiritual application can be found in Paul's words to the Thessalonians, "And the very God of peace sanctify you wholly; and I pray God your whole spirit and soul and body be preserved blameless unto the coming of our Lord Jesus Christ. Faithful is he that calleth you, who also will do it" (1 Thess. 5:23-24). It is possible to serve God in holiness and righteousness before Him "all the days of our life."

WILLIAM M. GREATHOUSE

General Superintendent

Converted during a six-week home mission campaign in Jackson, Tenn., Dr. Greathouse, at the age of 16, joined the Church of the Nazarene in 1935. He entered the experience of heart holiness during a season of spiritual awakening at Trevecca Nazarene College. From 1938 to 1958 he developed his combined abilities as pastor, scholar, and teacher. During these 20 years he completed degrees at Lambuth College, Trevecca Nazarene College, and Vanderbilt University; pastored Tennessee churches at Jackson, Franklin, Nashville (Immanuel), and Clarksville; and from 1955 to 1958 served as dean of religion and professor of Bible and theology at Trevecca Nazarene College while continuing his graduate study at Vanderbilt.

In 1958 Dr. Greathouse accepted the pastorate at Nashville First Church where he served until his election as president of Trevecca Nazarene College in 1963. In 1968 he accepted the presidency of the Nazarene Theological Seminary. Dr. Greathouse was elected to the Board of General Superintendents in 1976.

Dr. Greathouse is married to the former Ruth Nesbitt. They have three children: Mark Greathouse of Greensburg, Ky.; Rebecca Martin, Mount Juliet, Tenn.; and Elizabeth Sykes, Roswell, Ga.

THE PRAYER OF JESUS

SCRIPTURE: John 17

TEXT: *Sanctify them . . . that the world may know* (vv. 17, 23).

This high-priestly prayer of our Lord has been called the New Testament holy of holies. Indeed it is, for here Jesus, on the eve of His crucifixion, pulls back the veil of His soul as He unburdens His heart in petition and intercession.

First, He prays for himself: "Father, the hour has come; glorify thy Son that the Son may glorify thee" (v. 1, RSV).* The hour has come for the Son to be glorified in His death and the victory that crowned it.

Because God is love, the Cross is the glory of God— the perfection and triumph of His love, making possible the gift of the Holy Spirit (John 7:39). "Grant Me the Ascension," Jesus prays, "that I may execute the work of Pentecost" (Godet).

The burden of Jesus' prayer, however, is for the Church. As the Aaronic high priest entered into the holiest place to offer up the blood of the victim, so our High Priest enters into the immediate presence of God to offer up His consecrated life in order that we might be sanc-

---

*Unless otherwise indicated, all Scripture quotations in this chapter are from the *Revised Standard Version of the Bible.*

tified. "Sanctify them," He prays for the Church, "that the world may know" (vv. 17, 23).

In respect to this prayer for the Church a clear distinction must be made. For the original apostles the prayer was indeed answered on the Day of Pentecost. For us, it remains unanswered until we exercise sanctifying faith.

For the first believers the prayer of Jesus was literally answered. Exalted at the Father's right hand, the glorified Jesus poured out the sanctifying Spirit upon the 120 in the Upper Room, "purifying their hearts by faith" (Acts 2:32-33; 15:9, KJV).

For us the prayer remains answered. "I do not pray for these only," we hear our Lord saying, "but also for those who believe in me through their word" (v. 20). This high-priestly prayer of our Lord is for the Church Universal. As we study this intercessory prayer of Jesus for the Church, we must recognize that He is here interceding to the Father for *us*—both individually and collectively, as members of His Body. And as we analyze it, we discover it is threefold in its substance.

1. First, Jesus prays for the *purification* of the Church, to preserve it from the evil one.
2. Second, He prays for the *perfection* of the Church in love, to make it one as God is one.
3. Finally, He prays for the *consecration* of the Church to His redemptive mission in the world.

I. First, Jesus Prays for the Church That It May Be Purified to Be God's Holy People in an Unholy World

"Holy Father, keep them in thy name, which thou hast given me . . . I do not pray that thou shouldst take

46

them out of the world, but that thou shouldst keep them from the evil one. They are not of the world, even as I am not of the world. Sanctify them" (vv. 11, 15-17).

To sanctify is to separate, *from* the earthly and sinful, *to* the heavenly and holy. Adam Clarke sees the Greek verb as meaning literally "to de-earth."[1] To be truly sanctified is to have the dross of sin removed from our natures, so that only pure love to God and others remains in our hearts. In this imagery the Lord promises through the prophet Isaiah: "I will . . . smelt away your dross . . . and remove all your alloy" (1:25). God gloriously fulfilled this promise for the prophet himself in his memorable Temple experience (chap. 6).

As the prophet Malachi proclaims the coming of Christ, he exclaims, "The messenger of the covenant in whom you delight, behold, he is coming, says the Lord of hosts. But who can endure the day of his coming, and who can stand when he appears? For he is like a refiner's fire and like fullers' soap; he will sit as a refiner and purifier of silver" (3:1-3).

This was the imagery employed by John the Baptist when he contrasted his baptism with that of Christ: "I baptize you with water for repentance, but he who is coming after me is mightier than I, whose sandals I am not worthy to carry; he will baptize you with the Holy Spirit and with fire" (Matt. 3:11). Commenting on this, Dr. George Buttrick explains: "The ancient refiner watched the silver in the crucible, and kept the flame burning until the base metal had all come to the top and been skimmed off, until all agitation had ceased, and until he could see his face in the silver as in a mirror. This is the parable of the refining fire" of Christ's baptism.[2]

47

Observe here, first Christ mines us from the earth as we respond to His gospel call, repent, believe, and are baptized with water. But He thus saves us *in order that He might sanctify us.* His saving purpose is not fulfilled until the refining baptism with the Holy Spirit has purged our hearts from the dross of remaining sin, until our souls reflect His own image in "pure love to God and man" (Wesley).

It is one thing to be taken out of the world; it is quite another to have the world taken out of us! Until we are truly sanctified, we are to some degree like the unsanctified Corinthians to whom Paul wrote, "You are still worldly. For since there is jealousy and quarreling among you, are you not worldly? Are you not acting like mere men?" (1 Cor. 3:3, NIV).

The appropriate prayer of every sanctified believer is that of Charles Wesley:

> *Oh, that in me the sacred fire*
> *Might now begin to glow,*
> *Burn up the dross of base desire,*
> *And make the mountains flow!*
>
> *Refining Fire, go through my heart!*
> *Illuminate my soul;*
> *Scatter Thy life through every part,*
> *And sanctify the whole.*
>
> *My steadfast soul, from falling free,*
> *Shall them no longer move;*
> *While Christ is all the world to me,*
> *And all my heart is love.*

48

II. *Second, Jesus Prays for His Church That It May Be Perfected in Love and Become One as God Is One*

"Holy Father, keep them in thy name, which thou hast given me, that they may be one, even as we are one. . . . The glory which thou hast given me I have given to them, that they may be one even as we are one, I in them and thou in me, that they may become perfectly one, so that the world may know" (vv. 11, 22-23).

Here we are given a glimpse into the central mystery of the Christian faith—the mystery of the Triune God, revealed as a fellowship of love. This is the glory of God. This is the meaning of the statement "God is *agapē*."

> *Glory to God in Trinity,*
> *Whose names have mysteries unknown:*
> *In essence one, in Persons three;*
> *A social nature, yet alone.*
>
> —Isaac Watts

The three Persons of the Godhead are distinct but not separate. Each is in all, and all are in each (John 14:8-11, 16-23). Thus God is not solitary but social in His being. The one God, who is holy love, is the perfect Pattern of all fellowship in love.[3]

From eternity, the Father has perfectly loved the Son, and the Son has perfectly loved the Father, with the Holy Spirit being the Bond and Outflow of that love. This is the glory of God that Christ gives to the Church.

Observe, this is the glory Christ *gives* His Church. It is the unity we *receive* when we are incorporated by the Spirit into Christ. "For by one Spirit we were all baptized into one body—Jews or Greeks, slaves or free—and all were made to drink of one Spirit" (1 Cor. 12:12).

In Christ now meet both East and West;
In Him meet South and North.
All Christly souls are one in Him
Throughout the whole wide earth.

—JOHN OXENHAM

This unity is an experiential reality we know in Christ. The unity for which Christ prays, and which He gives by the Spirit, is *spiritual* unity, analogous to the unity of the Father and the Son. The Father is active in the Son, and apart from the Father the Son can do nothing (John 14:10). Again, the Son is in the Father, eternally in the unity of the Godhead (1:1, 18). "The Father and the Son are one and yet remain distinct. [So] believers *are* one, *and are to be one,* in the Father and in the Son, distinct from God, yet abiding in God, and themselves the sphere of God's activity" (14:12, 23).[4]

But this precious unity and "hallowed fellowship as cannot otherwise be known" except in the Church of Jesus Christ[5] is not only Christ's *gift* to us; it is also His *command.* We must not miss this point. Unity is both Christ's gift to us through the Spirit as we are incorporated into His Body by the miracle of salvation *and* His command that we perfectly love one another through His sanctifying grace. "A new commandment I give to you, that you love one another; even as I have loved you, that you also love one another. By this all men will know that you are my disciples, if you have love for one another" (John 13:34-35).

The perfect love that is Christ's command and promise does not mean uniformity of thought but unity in spirit. I shall always remember the unity that characterized the official board of Nashville First Church of the Nazarene during the years of my pastorate there. The strong-minded men who made up that board represented varying professions and points of view, and at times debate would be vigorous as we groped for God's direction in a matter that concerned the church's welfare and ministry. But after the session these strong men would put their arms around one another and leave as one man in the love of Christ! Nothing ever disrupted their "unity of the Spirit in the bond of peace" (Eph. 4:3). This is the unity of true sanctification.

In his little book *Climbing on Top of Your Troubles,* Berge Najarian relates his conversion to Christ and his subsequent infilling with the Spirit. As he completely surrendered to Christ, he says, "My whole being was permeated and saturated with His love. I felt an inner cleansing and a deep settled peace that I never had before."

Then follows this dramatic testimony: "Up to that time I had been harboring an unforgiving and revengeful spirit toward the Turks who had burned to death my maternal grandfather and uncle in 1895. Also, in 1920 my 85-year-old paternal grandfather and my 13-year-old brother were ruthlessly butchered in that last major massacre in Turkey when my parents escaped. But that morning my unforgiving and revengeful spirit disappeared. I could now forgive the Turks and love them because of the sanctifying power of the Holy Spirit."

It is the prayer of Jesus that we all shall experience this sanctifying power of the spirit that permeates our hearts with God's perfect love. *Then* the Church will reflect the glory of God, *but only then.*

III. *Finally, Jesus Prays for the Church, That It May Be Consecrated to His Redemptive Mission in the World*

"Sanctify them in the truth; thy word is truth. As thou didst send me into the world, so I have sent them into the world. And for their sake I consecrate myself, that they also may be consecrated in truth" (vv. 17-19).

"As thou didst send me into the world, so I have sent them into the world." "The Church exists by mission," says Emil Brunner, "as fire exists by burning." When fire ceases to burn, it ceases to be. And when the Church loses its sense of mission, it ceases to be the Church and becomes only a social club or a sect of the Pharisees!

The Church *is* mission. Its very reason for being is to continue Christ's mission in the world. The Father consecrated the Son and sent Him into the world (John 10:36); so the Son would consecrate the Church and send it into the world. "And for their sake I consecrate myself," He prays here, "that they also may be consecrated in truth" (or, *truly* consecrated).

If you are bothered that the Greek verb is here translated "consecrate" rather than "sanctify," permit me to cite the authority of Dr. H. Orton Wiley. He once defended this translation in an article in the *Herald of Holiness* by pointing out that as there is a *human* consecration that precedes the work of entire sanctification, so there is a *divine* consecration that follows. Quoting our *Manual,* he urged that the fruit of true sanctification is "entire devotement to God, and the holy obedience of love made perfect."[6]

Several years ago, after the Tennessee district assembly, I preached on a Sunday morning to an excited, growing congregation of about 150 in the small town of Erin, Tenn., in Houston County, population 8,000. I could not believe this was the same church I had known 30 years earlier when I was pastor in nearby Clarksville.

Erin church had been organized as an independent holiness congregation in 1898. In 1906 it affiliated with J. O. McClurkan's Pentecostal Mission. In 1911 it became a part of the Church of the Nazarene and that year hosted General Superintendent Phineas F. Bresee and the Clarksville district assembly. Through the years, until 1978— 80 years after its birth—Erin remained a "good little church" of 40 to 50 members with an annual budget of less than $5,000.

Then in 1978 something dramatic happened. That year Pastor Bob Mitchell received 24 new Nazarenes. As this growth continued year after year the congregation enlarged its facilities, doubling its sanctuary, adding a lovely Sunday School fellowship annex and a new parking lot. Each dollar they raised for building and expanding their local church facilities they matched with a dollar for home missions, giving $14,000 for a new church in Selmer, $15,000 for the Black church in Memphis, and $55,000 for a new church in Pulaski! All the while the congregation was bathed with glory and growing. In these brief years they have added about 20 new families to the membership and developed an annual budget of well over $100,000!

When I read some of this in the *Tennessee Nazarene,* I immediately called Bob Mitchell on the telephone. "What on earth has happened in Erin, Bob?" I asked. After a moment of reflection, Bob replied, "Brother Greathouse, all I can say is, I was gripped by a vital concern."

"What do you mean?" I queried. "What I mean is, the words of Jesus to the apostles on the evening of His resurrection gripped me. 'As my Father hath sent me, even so send I you'" (John 20:21, KJV). Bob Mitchell began to preach this—and the church began to believe and act on it. The rest is history.

"The Church exists by mission as fire exists by burning."

The prayer of Jesus is for a sanctified church—

A holy people reflecting Christ in a sinful world
United in the perfect love of God
Truly consecrated to His redemptive mission in the world

CHRISTIAN PERFECTION

SCRIPTURE: Matthew 22:34-40

John Wesley stands in the same relation to the doctrine of Christian perfection, or entire sanctification, as Martin Luther to that of justification by faith. The English reformer restored the neglected truth of evangelical perfection to its proper place in a Protestant understanding of the gospel.

When asked what he meant by Christian perfection, Wesley replied, "Loving God with all our heart, mind, soul, and strength. This implies that no wrong temper, none contrary to love, remains in the soul; and that all the thoughts, words, and actions are governed by pure love."[1]

In a sermon on this subject he declared, "It means perfect love. It is love excluding sin; love filling the heart, taking up the whole capacity of the soul. . . . How strongly [does this] imply the being saved from all sin! For as long as love takes up the whole heart, what room is there for sin therein?"[2]

To be perfect in this sense of the New Testament word[3] is not to be faultless but to answer to the end for which God created us. The pen with which I am writing is thus perfect. It "answers to the end" for which it was made: It writes satisfactorily, as long as I keep it filled with ink! So as Christians we are perfect, not if we are infallible and without fault, but if, filled with the Holy Spirit, we are conformed to the end for which we were created: namely, *"To glorify God and enjoy Him forever."*[4]

In our passage Jesus defines the New Testament rule of perfection: "Love God supremely and neighbor as self." "On these two commandments hang all the law and the prophets." This love is both the sum of God's requirement and the essence of His law for human nature. Perfect love is the substance of Bible religion.

"Whether you eat or drink, or whatever you do, do *all* to the glory of God" (1 Cor. 10:31, RSV, italics added). God's glory was the end for which we were made. So perfection is singleness of heart, purity of intention, simplicity of design—doing all "with an eye single to the glory of God."

55

And "Blest are the single-hearted, for they shall see God" (Matt. 5:8, *New American Bible*). Again, "If . . . thine eye be single, thy whole body shall be full of light" (6:22). This beatific vision is the soul's true fulfillment and happiness!

Love then is the distilled essence of Christian perfection. "The end of the commandment is love out of a pure heart, and a good conscience, and faith unfeigned." Love flowing from a pure heart, governed by a good conscience, and nourished by sincere faith is the *one grand aim* of "all the law and the prophets." "From which some having missed the mark, are turned aside to vain jangling" (1 Tim. 1:5, 6, Wesley's trans.).

"If you look for anything but more love," Wesley warns, "you are looking wide of the mark, you are getting off the royal way. And when you are asking others, 'Have you received this or that blessing?' if you mean anything but more love, you mean wrong. . . . Settle it then in your heart, that from the moment God has saved you from all sin, you are to aim at nothing more, but more of the love described in the thirteenth of Corinthians. You can go no higher than this, till you are carried into Abraham's bosom."[5]

I. *Perfection and Sin*

Now, if the essence of the law's requirement is love, the essence of sin is "missing the mark" of "pure love to God and man."

The problem, however, is not that we are poor marksmen; rather, we have picked the wrong target—self instead of God—and hit it perfectly!

Created looking directly to God as our last End, we have fallen off from God and turned into ourselves. "Now this [implies] a total apostasy and universal corruption in man," Wesley observes; "for where the last end is changed, there can be no real goodness. And this is the case of all men in their natural state: They seek not God, but themselves. Hence though many fair shreds of morality are among them, yet 'there is none that doeth good, no, not one.' For though some of them 'run well,' they are still off the way; *they never aim at the right mark.* Whithersoever they move, they cannot move beyond the circle of self. They seek themselves, they act for themselves; their natural, civil, and religious actions, from whatever spring they come, do all run into, and meet in, this dead sea" (italics added).[6]

Paul's account of this universal Fall and apostasy is vividly recounted in Romans 1. Refusing to glorify God as God, our foolish hearts have become darkened. Exchanging the truth of God for "the lie" of the serpent, we now worship and serve "the creature rather than the Creator, who is blessed for ever!" (vv. 18-25, RSV).

"For this reason" (RSV) God has given us up to "vile affections" and "a reprobate mind" (vv. 26-32). Turning from God as the Source of life and happiness, we have opened a moral vacuum in human nature and created "a void this world cannot fill."

57

The predicament of our fallen condition is that we are by nature "curved in on ourselves" (Luther). Self has been substituted for God, and we shall never be saved until we return to Him as our true End. As Augustine so truly wrote, "Thou hast made us for thyself, and our souls are restless till they rest in Thee." Only God can cleanse and fill the heart He has made for himself. And only then are we truly saved and made whole.

II. *Perfection and Conversion*

Our salvation, therefore, is in our "conversion"—our turning from self, the false end, to God, the true End and Center of our existence.

Isaiah most clearly issues this call, saying, "Seek ye the Lord while he may be found, call ye upon him while he is near: let the wicked forsake his way, and the unrighteous man his thoughts: and *let him return unto the Lord,* and he will have mercy upon him; and to our God, for he will abundantly pardon" (55:6-7, italics added).

"Conversion" is the right word—from "con," *with,* and "verto," *I turn.* We must return to God. We are able to turn, however, only with His gracious assistance. As Augustine put it, "Without God, we cannot; without us, He will not." Thank God, "while he is near" we *may* turn and be saved! And "he will abundantly pardon."

Sometimes in the first blush of a dramatic conversion a new convert may feel God has completely resolved the sin problem. I recall one of my students urging in all sincerity that God had entirely sanctified her at the time

58

of her conversion. Rather than argue with her I said, "Congratulations! You are the first person I have ever heard of who could give such a testimony. In examining hundreds of his Methodists John Wesley couldn't find a single person who was perfected in love at the time of justification." Some months later she came to my office acknowledging her need to be sanctified wholly. In her honesty she discovered what every believer sooner or later finds, that while the *reign* of sin is broken in conversion, its *remains* still plague the heart and call for a deeper purging.

What we painfully discover about ourselves in time, as newborn Christians, is that while we now have the mind of Christ, the old self-centered self is not dead. Though subdued, this self continues to fight and at times seeks to maintain its position against the Lordship of Christ.

This remaining egocentricity inevitably manifests itself in pride, envy, jealousy, lust, anger, and such sins of the spirit. To attack these manifestations only is a losing battle, for "what gets your attention gets you." *The problem to be resolved is the self problem.* Sins of the spirit, says E. Stanley Jones, all root back into an unsurrendered and uncleansed self the way our fingers root back into our hands. We are not *fully* converted, therefore, until we can say with Paul, "My present life is not that of the old 'I,' but the living Christ within me" (Gal. 2:20, Phillips). This is to be truly Christian, which in Dietrich Bonhoeffer's words means "to have the precise space once occupied by the old self to be occupied by Jesus Christ."

III. *Perfection by Faith*

The most important question any Christian can ask is this: How may I be made perfect in love? Since God commands us to love Him with all our heart and neighbor as self, can we call ourselves Christian if we disregard the Great Commandment? The requirement of perfect love is *not optional;* it is imperative for the believer who would obey God.

How then may I be perfected in love? "Repent and believe the gospel," Wesley answers. As there is a repentance and faith necessary to *initial* salvation, so there is a repentance and faith necessary to *full* salvation.

Let us be sure we understand what Wesley means by "the repentance of believers." The repentance requisite to saving faith involves a sense of guilt. Not so with the repentance of believers. This second repentance is the painful awareness of *inward* sin—a penitent acknowledgment of the remaining core of self-love that blocks the flow of the Spirit through us. Thank God, "There is therefore now no condemnation for those who are in Christ Jesus" (Rom. 8:1, RSV)—even for remaining sin! *Nevertheless,* if we yearn to be holy as God is holy, we cannot excuse the double-mindedness and divided loyalty that mar our devotion to God and truth. We must feel the conviction of the Spirit that moves us to cry out with the Psalmist, "Behold, thou desirest truth in the inward parts . . . Create in me a clean heart, O God; and renew a right spirit within me" (51:6, 10).

This repentance the prophet Isaiah experienced when, overwhelmed with the sense of God's holiness, he exclaimed, "Woe is me! for I am undone; because I am a man of unclean lips, and I dwell in the midst of a people of* unclean lips: for mine eyes have seen the King, the Lord of hosts" (6:5).

How desperately we need this vision of God's holiness if we are to truly see ourselves and exercise sanctifying faith!

But what is the faith by which we are entirely sanctified and perfected in love?

First, says Wesley, it is "the divine evidence and conviction"[7] that God has promised in Scripture to sanctify us wholly. Until this conviction is ours, we will never move one step further in our pursuit of holiness. But this very thing He promises: "And the Lord thy God *will* circumcise thine heart, and the heart of thy seed, to love the Lord thy God with all thine heart, and with all thy soul, that thou mayest live" (Deut. 30:6, italics added).

Second, it is the divine evidence and conviction that what God has promised He is able also to perform. Hear His Word: "And the very God of peace sanctify you wholly [NIV: "through and through"]; and I pray God your whole spirit and soul and body be preserved blameless unto the coming of our Lord Jesus Christ. *Faithful is he that calleth you, who also will do it*" (1 Thess. 5:23-24, italics added). The adverb translated "wholly," found only here in the New Testament, is a compound adverb[8] giving the promise the force: "The very God of peace sanctify you *entirely* so that you may be *perfect.*" Perfect in love.

Third, it is the divine evidence and conviction that what God has promised He is able and willing to do *now.* "Behold, now is the time. Today is the day of salvation" (see 2 Cor. 6:2). God doesn't need another moment. He is able and willing to sanctify you *now!*

Finally, it is the divine evidence and conviction that He *does* it! To the believing soul there comes a blessed moment when the assurance is given, that *the work is done!*[9]

> *The cleansing stream, I see, I see!*
> *I plunge and, oh, it cleanseth me!*
> —PHOEBE PALMER KNAPP

What God *commands* in the law He *gives* in the gospel! Not absolute perfection, but perfect love. "Then will I sprinkle clean water upon you, and ye shall be clean: from all your filthiness, and from all your idols, will I cleanse you. A new heart also will I give you, and a new spirit will I put within you: and I will take away the stony heart out of your flesh, and I will give you an heart of flesh. And I will put my spirit within you, and cause you to walk in my statutes, and ye shall keep my judgments, and do them" (Ezek. 36:25-27).

O for a heart to praise my God,
  A heart from sin set free,
A heart that always feels Thy blood
  So freely shed for me!

A heart resigned, submissive, meek,
  My great Redeemer's throne,
Where only Christ is heard to speak,
  Where Jesus reigns alone.

Oh, for a lowly, contrite heart,
  Believing, true, and clean,
Which neither life nor death can part
  From Him that dwells within!

A heart in ev'ry thought renewed,
  And full of love divine;
Perfect, and right, and pure, and good—
  A copy, Lord, of Thine!
                    —CHARLES WESLEY

JERALD D. JOHNSON

General Superintendent

Jerald Johnson (identified more readily by his friends as Jerry) hails from the state of Nebraska. His father pastored in that state during a lifetime of ministerial service for the Church of the Nazarene. Jerry was born in a parsonage (literally) in Curtis but spent most of his childhood and young teen years in York. It was here under his parents' influence that he came to know the Lord Jesus as His Savior.

While a senior at Northwest Nazarene College at Nampa, Idaho, Jerry came to experience the blessing of entire sanctification. He remembers vividly the encounter he had with God and the moment of full surrender that resulted in a clean heart and a motivation for service that he still experiences today.

This service has taken him through four pastorates in the United States, 11 years on the continent of Europe as pioneer pastor-superintendent, 7 years as World Mission administrator, and now nearly 7 years as a general superintendent.

He and his wife, Alice, have four children (three sons and one daughter) and four grandchildren. The Johnsons make their home in Overland Park, Kans.

SINCE WE HAVE THESE PROMISES

SCRIPTURE: 2 Corinthians 6:14—7:1

TEXT: 7:1

"Since we have these promises" (NIV).* What promises do we have?

In the closing verses of the chapter just preceding the text, Paul has been quoting from the Old Testament. These quotes contain three wonderful promises. The first is in verse 16, "As God has said: 'I will live with them and walk among them, and I will be their God, and they will be my people.'"

This is God speaking to a people who had come to acknowledge Him as God. Consequently they would be blessed with His presence. Life for them would be different because of this change that had taken place. How pleasant and reassuring to know God would be at the center of life's activity.

This promise we too may claim. The turnaround in life, the change that takes place when one turns to Him gives assurance of His presence and leadership at the very core of living. We have a theological term explaining this change. It is called "regeneration." It is, however, more

------

*All Scripture quotations in this chapter are from *The Holy Bible, New International Version.*

than a theological term; it is a marvelous expression of God's grace and mercy that in effect says that life can be different from the way it now is. One can be changed from what one was before.

Have you claimed this promise?

The second word of assurance is found in verse 17 of chapter 6, another of Paul's quotes from the Old Testament. This reads simply, "I will receive you."

Again, this is God speaking. The implied word is that in spite of sins that may have been committed, He will receive us. This is possible because of the death of His Son, Jesus, and the Atonement for sins provided. Evil deeds committed are forgiven, the slate is declared clean, the burden of guilt is lifted, and *He receives us.*

In this case the theological term describing the experience is "justification." However, it is again more than a theological term; it is a marvelous expression of God's grace and mercy making it possible to be received into His presence as forgiven Christians.

Have you claimed this wonderful promise?

The third promise is found in verse 18, chapter 6. Again it is a quote from the Old Testament. "I will be a Father to you, and you will be my sons and daughters, says the Lord Almighty."

God is now saying that although you may have been on the outside looking in, you may now be on the inside looking out. No longer are you an alien or a stranger, but you become an actual member of God's family. The theological term describing what takes place here is "adoption"; but again, it is an expression of love and mercy beyond description that permits us to be included in God's inner circle. The new relationship is intimate and close.

He is our Father, and we actually become His sons and daughters.

Have you claimed this promise?

All three experiences take place at one and the same time when there is true repentance for sin and Christ is received as Lord and Savior. There is a radical change in life. Sins are forgiven, and the adoption into God's family is declared. It's called being "born again," becoming a Christian, belonging to the Lord. These great and marvelous promises are to be accepted and treasured.

Have you claimed these promises?

"Since we have these promises," Paul continued, "let us purify ourselves from everything that contaminates body and spirit." The promises having been claimed, the Christian now begins to build a life that is according to God's plan and purpose with these promises as a foundation upon which such a life is constructed. Therefore, the challenge to "purify ourselves from everything that contaminates body and spirit." This challenge prompts two important questions to be raised. The first is, what contaminates the body? The second question is, what contaminates the spirit?

For answers to these questions we need once again to refer to Paul's quotes from the Old Testament recorded in the concluding verses of 2 Corinthians, chapter 6. Verse 17 contains answers to both questions.

Again, the first question is, what contaminates the body? In verse 17 of chapter 6 we read, "Touch no unclean thing." "Things" contaminate bodies, and for the believer such things are not to be touched.

Prior to verse 17 Paul has used a favorite illustration of his. He says in verse 16, "For we are the temple of the living God." We all understand that temples built for the worship of God are dedicated to Him for that purpose. From the day of dedication on, there are some things simply not allowed to take place in a temple that now belongs to Him.

The application of the illustration is very clear. Our bodies are also to be dedicated to Him. They shall become temples of the Holy Spirit. Therefore, "things" shall not be allowed to contaminate these temples. How do we understand this? The answer would be simply as follows. The ears shall not listen to "things" that might contaminate the temple. Neither shall the eyes look on "things" that could contaminate the temple. Likewise, the mouth shall not be a receptacle for "things" that would contaminate. The feet shall not be allowed to take the temple to places where there are "things" that might contaminate. The Bible admonition is understandable: "Touch no unclean thing."

The second question then to be answered is, what contaminates the spirit? The Bible speaks of body, soul, and spirit—the latter being the presentation of ourselves as others see us. This speaks of attitude, bearing, as well as manner of speech.

Now the quote from the Old Testament in chapter 6 and verse 17 that answers the question relative to that which could contaminate the spirit is, "Come out from them and be separate." The word "them" speaks of people. People contaminate the spirit. This is especially so when the people are negative, when they are critical, or when they are sinful. To avoid a contamination of the spirit the admonition is to come out from "them."

One might well ask, how is it possible to "come out from them" when one lives with "them," works with "them," or goes to school with "them"? Perhaps we can find the answer in the prayer recorded in John, chapter 17. This is the prayer of Jesus in which He said, "They are not of the world any more than I am of the world. My prayer is not that you take them out of the world but that you protect them from the evil one. They are not of the world, even as I am not of it" (vv. 14-16). The directive is clearly defined, and the plan of God is understandable. Of course, we may live with "them." We may work with "them," and even go to school with "them." Yet, by God's grace and the strength He imparts to us, it is possible to so live that we influence "them" rather than they influencing us. The directive is, therefore, fulfilled, "Come out from them."

Now, Paul moves on to an important step in the Christian's development after having claimed "these promises." The text reads again, "Since we have these promises, dear friends, let us purify ourselves from everything that contaminates body and spirit, *perfecting holiness* out of reverence for God" (italics added).

The words "perfecting holiness," as used here, speak of something that happens. This is a reference to something that takes place. It is that which one may know and experience. Again, there is a theological term to describe this experience. It is "sanctification." It is more, however, than a theological term; it is also a clearly defined biblical term. Again, it is a further expression of God's grace, of His mercy, and of His power that provides for the cleansing of all sin from the heart. Committed sins are forgiven. In the perfection of holiness, however, the original sin

69

that prompted sins to be committed in the first place is cleansed completely because of the full provision of Christ's death.

Jesus prayed, "Sanctify them by the truth; your word is truth" (John 17:17).

Paul insisted, "It is God's will that you should be sanctified" (1 Thess. 4:3).

The Hebrews writer assured us in chapter 13, verse 12, "And so Jesus also suffered outside the city gate to make the people holy through his own blood."

The promises having been claimed and the commitment made to a life pleasing to Him, the experience of holiness perfected in an act of grace is awaiting the obedient servant of Christ. The question, then, to be raised is fair and logical. Since you have these promises, have you been sanctified? Is this an experience to which you have a clear testimony? Does He sanctify you just now?

The expression "perfecting holiness," as used here, speaks not only of something that happens and, likewise, that which one may know and experience, but it also speaks of process. It's not just an experience of a moment, but it is a continuing experience of cleansing and growth in God's grace. Having been sanctified, one continues to follow God in a close relationship that allows for improvement as one endeavors to become more like Christ himself. With the heart cleansed from all sin, there is a sensitivity to the Holy Spirit's teaching and directing as mistakes are corrected, attitudes improved, and the life of holiness generally perfected. This is a process to be continued throughout the living of a sanctified life. It becomes true that every day with Jesus is sweeter than the day before. Our lives are not only pleasing to Him but pleasing to others as well.

Relevance to the singing of the devotional hymn is underscored.

Oh, to be like Thee! Oh, to be like Thee,
Blessed Redeemer, pure as Thou art!
Come in Thy sweetness, come in Thy fullness;
Stamp Thine own image deep on my heart.

There is a great story recorded in 2 Kings 4:8-10. The prophet Elisha is known to frequent a village named Shunem. We are told that a "well-to-do woman was there, who urged him to stay for a meal. So whenever he came by, he stopped there to eat." One day this wealthy lady spoke to her husband of a plan whereby they would build a room on top of the house. They would place in it a bed, a table, a chair, and a lamp. This would be known as the prophet's chamber. Her intention was that she and her husband would invite Elisha to stay in this room whenever he visited their village. This is what she said of the prophet: "I know that this man who often comes our way is a holy man of God." One can only conclude that she desired this prophet to be in their home as his presence would be a blessing to the entire family. The visits of a "holy man of God" would be a permeating influence that could only be beneficial to all. Should it not be that way with all of us? As we claim His promises, live as He wants us to live, allowing Him to sanctify and cleanse us from all sin, we will grow and develop in grace in a way that makes holiness attractive and even welcome to a watching world.

What great promises we have. What great prospects are ours. Let us read it again and give special attention to

71

its meaning as it applies to each one of us wherever we might be in our journey of faith.

"Since we have these promises, dear friends, let us purify ourselves from everything that contaminates body and spirit, perfecting holiness out of reverence for God."

MARK OF SPIRITUALITY

SCRIPTURE: 1 Corinthians 3:1-17

First Corinthians is a letter addressed to a church congregation. Many congregations today would be able to identify with these Corinthian Christians. That they were Christians we need not be in doubt.

In the first place Paul addressed them as "brethren" (v. 1). This was a clear identification of their standing in the family of God. We recognize brothers and sisters of the same family. For those outside the family circle we use other titles or other means of address. Inside, we readily acknowledge the relationship. This was obviously Paul's intent in speaking to his "brethren." He was a son of God, and he knew that they too were children of the Lord. They, therefore, had much in common, for they had one Heavenly Father. It is a relationship that only those who are truly children of God fully understand. Because these Corinthians understood, and he also understood, their commonality was recognized; and, therefore, the greeting "brethren."

Also Paul recognized them as being believers. He spoke of himself and Apollos as "ministers by whom he believed" (v. 5). The implication is that this was more than a mere superficial acknowledgment of God as a Supreme Being or a mere assent to the Lordship of His Son, Jesus. Genuine faith goes beyond such and makes it very personal. A true believer will not just acknowledge the gift of God's Son to the world but states, "God sent Jesus to this world for *me.*" This carries through the basic tenets of faith until the believer declares, "Jesus died *for me.* He arose from the grave *for me.* He makes intercession in heaven *for me;* and He's coming back to *receive me* unto himself, that where He is I may be also."

In American culture we will often identify such a one as a "Christian." In many parts of the world "Christian," however, has such a broad interpretation, even a political one, that the distinctive is further made among "Christians" as to who is a "believer" and who is not. Obviously Paul acknowledged these Corinthians as being true *believers.*

Another identification of Paul's as related to these Corinthians was the expression he used in verse 1, "in Christ." There is a marked difference between being "in Christ" or "outside of Christ." They had by God's grace crossed that boundary. Not of those who were outside of Christ and likewise outside of grace, they were a part of the inner circle. They were "in Christ."

The paradox of all of this is that although these people were "brethren," "believers," and "in Christ," Paul bluntly said to them that they weren't spiritual. They were not, in other words, all God intended them to be. Hindering factors that would jeopardize their standing as "spiritual" Christians were obvious, so Paul suggested that they were "carnal" (v. 3).

This strong charge would demand justification for it to be made, and Paul was prepared to further explain. He makes some comparisons between spirituality and adulthood. You are "babes in Christ" (v. 1), he said. At least there were strong indications of childhood in what he had observed.

For one thing, Paul had desired to give them meat of the Word (cf. Heb. 5;12-14). Only adults can chew and digest meat. Babies cannot. They had not been able to receive what he had offered them. Instead he found it necessary to restrict them to a spiritual milk diet: "I have fed you with milk, and not with meat" (v. 2).

Furthermore, their behavior reflected childhood characteristics that Paul was quick to identify as being "carnal." He wrote, "Whereas there is among you envying, and strife, and divisions, are ye not carnal . . . ?" (v. 3).

Envying, strife, and divisions are the marks of children. One child sees a toy another has and desires it greatly. Desire forces the child to endeavor to secure the toy for his own. The owner, however, isn't ready to give up his possession and clings tenaciously to it. The result is "strife." Then Mother must intervene and send one child to one room and the other child to another room. That's "division." Envying, strife, divisions reflect behavior we may patiently tolerate in children. It is tragic, however, when it is demonstrated in adults. This is especially so when it is in adults who profess to be Christians. It may be more sophisticated and even subtle, yet similar indeed.

Envy for position, even in the church, can lead to words being spoken that reflect a carnal spirit. Divisions among people of a congregation will more likely than not stem from a carnal and certainly not a spiritual people.

Paul was obviously greatly distressed over what was happening in this congregation. He pled for change, doing so by establishing what true spirituality is as a goal to be attained. He answers three central questions for us. First, he tells us who is a spiritual Christian; second, he tells us what a spiritual Christian knows; and third, he tells us what a spiritual Christian does.

First, who is a spiritual Christian? Here's the clue in verse 9: "labourers together." Laboring or working "together" with others is a true mark of a spiritual Christian. There is no place for self-exaltation, a "go it alone" attitude here. Within the Body of Christ the spiritual Christian joins hands with brothers and sisters in the Lord, contributing his means, talents, and time to support the total work of God. Position seeking is not part of the pattern. Personal demands for attention are never allowed to surface. The total contribution is for harmony, peace, and productivity in the Kingdom. Spiritual Christians are "labourers together."

The second question Paul answers is what a spiritual Christian knows. Verse 16 reads, "Know ye not that ye are the temple of God, and that the spirit of God dwelleth in you?" The implication is clear. Spiritual Christians know they are the temples of God's Spirit. He, the Holy Spirit, is the Third Person of the Triune Godhead who possesses those who have allowed Him to do so. The spiritual Christian acknowledges His residence in His temple and reflects obeisance to Him in speech, thought, and behavior.

The life-style will demonstrate respect for the One who dwells in His temple. Spiritual Christians know this and allow His presence to permeate and direct their daily living for God.

The final question Paul answers is what a spiritual Christian does. Verse 10 reveals to us the answer to this question: "as a wise masterbuilder." The answer, simply put, is a spiritual Christian *builds*.

Not everyone fits in the construction business. Some of us would have no skills whatsoever when it comes to erecting a building. At the same time, some of us, however, would probably know how to tear something down.

The presence of carnality is negative and defeating. It is useful for tearing down. This is, of course, in reference to activity within the Body of Christ. Spirituality, on the other hand, is positive and constructive. Spiritual Christians *build*.

Some very interesting building materials are alluded to in this scripture. There are six of them: "gold, silver, precious stones, wood, hay, stubble" (v. 12). It is difficult to see how these six could possibly mix together to contribute toward any kind of a useful structure. They probably don't, and there is undoubtedly a reason why Paul states that "every man's work shall be made manifest . . . because it shall be revealed by fire" (v. 13).

In the Gospel of Matthew we find another reference to fire. In chapter 3, verse 11, we hear John the Baptist preaching in the wilderness prophesying the coming of Jesus: "I indeed baptize you with water unto repentance: but he that cometh after me . . . shall baptize you with the Holy Ghost, and with fire."

Carnal Christians need the baptism of the Holy Ghost and fire. Indeed, fire is one of the symbols used in scripture to describe the Holy Ghost himself. His baptism is a cleansing, burning, sanctifying process that takes care of that which is called "carnal" and prepares a temple where He may indeed and in fact reside in all of His fullness.

How many "brethren," "believers," and those "in Christ" who are endeavoring to live for God find themselves falling short of spiritual standards—because they are yet "carnal"? It is for just such the promise is given. The coming of our Lord Jesus Christ, the sacrifice He made on the Cross has made it possible to receive the baptism of the Holy Ghost and fire.

When fire is applied to the construction of wood, hay, stubble, gold, silver, and precious stones, the inevitable will happen. The wood, hay, and stubble will burn up, and what is left over will be gold, silver, and precious stones.

When the fires of God in the baptism of the Holy Ghost and fire are applied to the carnal Christian, the inevitable will take place. Envy, strife, and divisions will be burnt up, and that which will remain will be a spiritual, a sanctified Christian, a true temple of the Holy Ghost. May it happen in your life.

JOHN A. KNIGHT

General Superintendent

Born in Texas, John A. Knight was converted as a boy, sanctified wholly as a teenager, and answered the call to preach as a student at Bethany-Peniel College, where he graduated in 1952.

After earning a graduate degree in philosophy from the University of Oklahoma, Dr. Knight became the first pastor of a home mission church in Columbia, Tenn. Simultaneously he enrolled in Vanderbilt University, where he earned the bachelor of divinity degree and the Ph.D. in theology.

His pastoral ministry was directed to four churches in Tennessee, the last one being Nashville Grace Church of the Nazarene in 1972. He was professor of Bible and theology at Trevecca Nazarene College, Mount Vernon Nazarene College, and Bethany Nazarene College.

In 1972 he made the transition from the classroom to the presidency of Mount Vernon Nazarene College and in 1976 moved to the presidency of Bethany Nazarene College. For a short interim period between the two administrative positions, he served as editor of the *Herald of Holiness.*

Dr. Knight was a member of the General Board from 1980 to 1985 and was elected 25th general superintendent of the Church of the Nazarene in Anaheim, Calif., June 1985.

He is married to the former Justine Rushing. The Knights have three children, John Allan, Jr., James, and Judith Ann.

ALL LOVES EXCELLING

1 John 4:10-21 (v. 17)
Introduction

God's love is the *definition* and *declaration* of pure love, by which all loves are to be evaluated and measured. It has been poured out on unworthy man, and demonstrated in the propitiation for man's sins (v. 10).

The love of God in Christ "shed abroad in our hearts by the Holy [Spirit]" (Rom. 5:5; also see Titus 3:4-6) is the example that man is to emulate in all his personal and social relationships. This love alone is the *source* and *power* of all other loves.

John Wesley equated this love of God in man with holiness and holy living. He taught that "Christian perfection," or "perfect love," is "loving God with all the heart, soul, mind, and strength, and one's neighbor as oneself."

The validity of Wesley's judgment is borne out by the passage before us. The purpose of the entire Epistle is seen in such expressions as: "that ye may know that ye have eternal life" (5:13); "that ye sin not" (2:1); "that your joy may be full" (1:4). John's aim is to direct believers into the *fullness* of God's love. He does this by portraying his vision of Christian holiness, which is perfect love for God and man.

This Epistle, then, is one of love, holiness, and the victorious life. It reflects a deep, vital union with God emphasizing true holiness and righteousness. The disciple whom Jesus loved combines his understanding of *life in God* and the *life of perfect love* with the *fullness of the Spirit.*

Chapter 4, verse 17, and the surrounding verses, present to Christ's followers the biblical standard of *perfect love* revealed in and made possible by Jesus Christ. The emphasis is not so much on the stages or crises of faith and experience through which one passes to come to this degree of maturity; but rather on the quality of life that results from the divine activity exercised in saving and sanctifying grace. What we have here is a description of the life of holiness and of the possibilities of Christlikeness through the fullness of the indwelling Spirit.

Our passage of Scripture clearly describes and reflects the character of one whose love has been *made perfect.* In these 12 verses the word "love" is used 22 times. The English word "love" translates two different words in the New Testament that convey different meanings. One *(agapē)* is used primarily to refer to God's love and refers to a deep and constant love that is not dependent upon the merit of its object. The other *(philia)* represents the tender affection between two human beings. In all 22 instances the former word is used. Thus we are talking about God's kind of love.

Three tests of divine life or perfect love are put forward in John's Epistle:

1. Whether we believe that Jesus is the Son of God— by the commitment of our will

80

2. Whether we are living lives of righteousness—moral and ethical uprightness

3. Whether we have love one for another—even for our enemies

When asked, "Is there any example in Scripture of persons who have attained perfect love?" Wesley replied: "Yes, St. John and all those of whom he speaks in 1 John 4:17."

Let us look at the way the apostle of love views a "true" Christian, one who is filled with perfect love. May we ask ourselves: Do we love with a love made perfect—with the very love of Christ? And may we pray with Charles Wesley:

> Love divine, **all loves excelling,**
>> Joy of heav'n, to earth come down!
> Fix in us Thy humble dwelling;
>> All Thy faithful mercies crown.
> Jesus, Thou art all compassion;
>> Pure, unbounded love Thou art.
> Visit us with Thy salvation;
>> Enter ev'ry trembling heart.
>>>> (emphasis added)

I. *Perfect Love Excels in the Fellowship It Preserves (1:3-7)*

First John has all the marks of a sermon, the work of a pastor who seeks to build up his people in the faith. The author employs graphic contrasts—light and darkness, life and death, saint and sinner, love and hate, Christ and Antichrist. These contrasts are practically synonymous, and any one of them may be substituted by almost any other. They can all be expressed in the phrase "fellowship and alienation." John is extolling "fellowship," the immediate union of the soul with God that issues in righteousness in all the relationships of one's life. Perfect love both creates and preserves this fellowship.

A. This Fellowship Is a Gift of God Through Jesus Christ (v. 10)

Sinful man cannot love God or have fellowship with Him ("Not that we loved God"). We were enemies to God, and yet Christ died for us. It was God's love, not our merit or our lovableness, that induced Him to devise means to accomplish our salvation.

"We love him, because he first loved us" (v. 19). God's love for man is not a response to our love. Our love depends upon, and is the result of, His love. Real love in its origin is not human but divine. Human love at best is only responsive; it is never original and spontaneous. The marvel of God's method with men is that He loves them into loving—both by His prevenient grace and by His tranforming grace. In this His love excels.

B. This Fellowship Is Made Possible by the Removal of Our Sins (v. 10)

The Father has "sent his Son to be the propitiation for our sins." The Greek word for "propitiation" is used only here and in 2:2, without reference to the one to whom it is offered. It should not be understood as an appeasement to God but as a reference to the personal means by whom God shows mercy to those who believe on Christ. Thus the word has been rendered an "atoning sacrifice" (NIV).

In and through Christ man finds mercy and forgiveness of his sins, pardon and peace with God. The alienation and estrangement that separated man from God are taken away. The guilt and power of sin that weighted down man and held him in bondage are gone. One is reconciled to God by Christ's death, a "new and living way" whereby we have access to the Father (Heb. 10:19-20). The pollution of sin, the spirit of selfishness that hinders growth in grace, is cleansed. In dealing effectively with the sin problem, God's perfect love excels.

C. This Fellowship Rests upon Confession of Christ as Savior and Lord (vv. 14-15)

The testimony described, "we have seen and do testify," expresses the common and abiding witness of the Church (cf. 1:1-5) as it is appropriated by the faith of each believer personally. The confession "that Jesus is the Son of God" is not merely the mental assent to, nor declaration of, a fact—even the devils have this kind of faith and "tremble" (James 2:19). Rather, it is the public recognition and acceptance of the person of Christ as the Divine Savior. It is submission to Him as Lord and trust in Him for salvation. He who with the heart thus acknowledges Him, and with the tongue confesses Him, receives Him and has eternal life (cf. Rom. 10:9-10).

"God dwelleth in him" who makes this confession, "and he in God" (v. 15). This reciprocal indwelling in God and in Christ implies the most intimate fellowship of the believer with the Father and with the Son, in whom He is revealed. The conditions of this fellowship are love, confession, and obedience. The effects are fruitfulness and acceptance. The sign is the possession of the Holy Spirit, who lavishes God's love in the heart and inspires the filial feeling, so that we may pray, "Abba, Father" (Rom. 8:15; Gal. 4:6). To so recognize the Father and His working, which is a result of God's grace, certifies true sonship.

Perfect love preserves this fellowship—in this it excels.

II. *Perfect Love Excels in the Assurance It Provides (v. 7)*

One cannot gain acceptance with God through good deeds or accumulated merit, by one's economic or racial background—but by grace alone through faith in Jesus Christ. The apostle Paul failed to find peace with God through his own righteousness. He was circumcised the eighth day, of the stock of Israel, of the tribe of Benjamin, a Hebrew of the Hebrews, a Pharisee. He zealously persecuted the Church, a virtue in the minds of the Jews. Regarding the law, he was blameless. His dependence upon these "virtues" only increased his guilt and magnified his spiritual paucity. But when he met Jesus Christ on the Damascus road and accepted His righteousness, his life was transformed, and he was accepted into "the beloved." He testified to the Philippians: "What things were gain to me, these I counted loss for Christ" (3:7).

A. God Assures That We Belong to Him by Giving His Spirit of Love (v. 13)

The Source of the Christian's assurance is the Gift of the Holy Spirit (see 3:24; also Rom. 8:15-16). Here is the Divine Presence whom Jesus said He would ask the Father to send His disciples and all His followers of every age (John 14:16). The Holy Spirit brings assurance to the Christian because the devil has been judged, and all who dwell in God, and God in him, share in the victory over evil (John 16:11).

The Holy Spirit is the Christian's proof of acceptance with God. His presence enables him to know that he belongs to God. The Spirit is the evidence of the fellowship of the community of Christ's Body, because all experience the same Presence. While the Holy Spirit respects and enhances each one's individuality, there is a oneness about His presence that assures each member of a common fellowship through Him. That oneness is the unity of their faith in Jesus Christ. This confession is prompted by the indwelling Spirit.

It is for this reason that the Spirit centers attention upon Jesus. When we say we "feel the Spirit," we mean we are sensing the presence of Christ. When the Spirit indwells us He enables us to exalt Christ, a confirmation that we belong to Him.

B. God Gives Assurance, or "Boldness," for the Day of Judgment—Through Christlikeness (v. 17)

To live in the love of God and have it flow out of us to others bears fruit in holy boldness. The fear of judgment fades because one sees in the person of our Judge Him who has died for us, regenerated our hearts, and fills us with himself. The writer of Hebrews expresses a virtually universal anxiety of mankind when he says that all men must die and after this face the judgment (9:27). Whether that judgment be the Great White Throne (Rev. 20:11-15), or the judgment of consequences in this life, it is a fearful thing.

85

The love of God in one's heart brings boldness because one knows the Judge of all is working out His purpose in one's life. This boldness comes because that one is becoming like Christ, the Standard by which all men are judged. What will be asked of the believer at the last is already occurring through the cleansing and empowering love of God in the heart and life of the child of God. The love of God makes one fearless of judgment, because judgment is that which is happening in the person in whom the love of God is perfected.

John firmly declares, "As he is"—pure, holy, loving —"so are we in this world" (v. 17)—saved from our sins, made like to himself in righteousness and true holiness. The ground of our boldness, then, is present likeness to Christ. Our essential likeness to Him is not in our trials, or persecutions, or sufferings, nor even primarily in the fact that we are not of the world as He is not of the world. Rather, it is in the fact that we are *righteous* as He is *righteous.* Our likeness is to Christ's character and spirit.

C. Perfect Love Casts Out Fear (v. 18)

There is "no fear in love" because fear pulls apart, while love unites. Love that is *perfect* casts out fear. Fear has to do with God's punishment and is an aspect of His discipline—"fear hath torment." The one who fears is not perfected in love and therefore shrinks away from God.

Bengel has said there are four classes of men:

1. Those who have *neither fear nor love*—the unregenerate and unconverted. They have no love for God and no fear of God.

2. Those who have *fear of God,* but *no love for Him*—the unregenerate but now convicted. They

86

have caught a glimpse of their sinfulness and are afraid.

3. Those who have *both fear and love*—the newly regenerated, babes in Christ, or young converts. They love God but still fear Him because of their inner uncleanness.

4. Those who have *only love for God*—Christians in whom the love of God is perfected. They have had their heart cleansed from all inward sin and have been sanctified wholly (to use our terminology).

Someone asked Dr. J. G. Morrison: "How much religion will a man have to have to make it to heaven?" He replied: "Enough that he feels comfortable in the presence of a holy God." That requires a holy heart.

"Perfect love casteth out fear."

We must not suppose that the love of God implanted in the heart of man is ever imperfect in itself; it is only so in degree. But there may be a lesser or greater degree of what is perfect in itself. So it is with respect to the love that the followers of Christ have. We are not to imagine that the love of God casts out *every* kind of fear from the soul—fear of falling from great heights, fear of fire, and so on. But perfect love does cast out that fear that has "torment"—fear of God himself. We stand in awe of Him and with reverence, but we do not cringe before Him in fear of capricious judgment.

The more one grows in the Christian graces the more other kinds of fear are removed. Fear of failure, fear that others will betray, fear of people's opinions. Such fears distort perspective, disrupt relationships, retard growth, and inhibit development. There are fears that blind moral judgment and inflame passions.

Love is positive; fear is negative. These are mutually exclusive. The more one loves, the less he fears. The more he fears, the less he loves. While some fears may have value, "There is nothing that fear does for us in a constructive way that love and confidence will not do better" (T. E. Martin). Perfect love enables us to accept each day and all that it brings in confidence and boldness. In this it excels.

III. *Perfect Love Excels in the Service It Promotes (vv. 7-8, 11, 20-21)*

A. *Love for Others Is Rooted in Love for God, or Love from God (v. 21)*

"If God so loved us, we ought also to love one another" (v. 11). We are to love those who are a part of the fellowship of believers. However, Jesus told the disciples that if they loved only those who loved them, they would have no reward (Matt. 5:46). This includes loving one's enemies and doing good to those who persecute us (Matt. 5:43-45). Loving others, even our enemies, is not so tall an order when we see the activity of God in us. The love we have for God and others comes from the indwelling presence of God. God dwells in those who love Him, and His love is perfected in them. Perfect love is the work of God in the heart of the believer. It is the nature of God not only to love but also to bring that love to perfection or fulfillment. Christian holiness is the fruit of the love relationship with God. It is what He intends for everyone born again of the Spirit.

The initiative, of course, is God's. We do not perfect His love in us; He does. When we open our hearts to the love of God in commitment, consecration, faith, and obedience, we are at one with the purpose for which we were created. We begin to be what we were intended to be. That intention is brought to fulfillment as His love is perfected in us. Having this perfection of love, one can see God. Jesus said, "Blessed are the pure in heart: for they shall see [enjoy] God" (Matt. 5:8). This perfection or purity of heart is an unselfish and giving love that does not love for return, but finds its joy in giving.

B. Hatred, or Unconcern for Others, Evidences a Lack of Perfect Love (v. 20)

John asks a pointed rhetorical question: If one does not love "his brother whom he hath seen, how can he love God whom he hath not seen?" The implication is that if a man fails in the duty of love to one with whom he is in daily interaction, he cannot perform the more difficult duty of loving one whom he has never seen, and whose existence is invisible to him except by the eye of faith. To this point, John has not directly mentioned our love for God. Now he brings it into sharp focus and insists that our love for God is validated by our love for others.

Loving others, with a love made perfect, is not an option but a commandment: "This commandment . . . That he who loveth God love his brother also" (v. 21). This may be a reference to the summary of the Mosaic law that calls for loving God with one's whole heart and one's neighbor as oneself (Lev. 19:18; Deut. 6:5; Matt. 22:37-39; Mark 12:30-31; Luke 10:27). The commandment is a commandment of love. Love, being of the very nature of God, contains its own motivation to self-expression toward others. It is of the nature of God's love in us to express itself. The proof that love is real, *perfected,* in the full Christian sense, lies in the overt action to which it leads. There is no real love for God that does not show itself in obedience to His commands—love being lived out to its "fingertips" in all segments of our society. In this perfect love excels.

Conclusion

The *beauty* of this passage of Scripture is rivaled only by 1 Corinthians 13—the "hymn of love." "God is love" (v. 16). He has made His love known to man through His Son, awakening man's echoing response, which is demonstrated in visible acts of service to others.

The question is: Has the *beauty* of this perfected love come to decorate our lives? Have we confessed our lack of love and consecrated our life to God? Do we in this moment love God with all our heart, soul, mind, and strength, and our neighbor (as well as enemies) as ourself?

If not, we can by His grace. His love can be implanted in our hearts by the fullness of the Holy Spirit. We may by faith receive Him who is Love, enabling and empowering us to love "because he first loved us."

"Herein is our love made perfect."
All other loves this love excels.

A CHRISTIAN'S CONFESSION

Mark 8:27—9:1

To be a Christian is to confess Christ. Jesus said: "Whosoever . . . shall *confess* me before men, him will I confess also before my Father which is in heaven" (Matt. 10:32). Paul declared: "If thou shalt *confess* with thy mouth the Lord Jesus, and shalt believe in thine heart that God hath raised him from the dead, thou shalt be saved. For with the heart man believeth unto righteousness; and with the mouth *confession* is made unto salvation" (Rom. 10:9-10, all italics added).

The Christian's confession moves through two major stages: (1) There is a confession that is genuine but is not made in full awareness of the implications involved. (2) There is a confession that both understands and submits to the implications.

These stages in the life of the Christian are clearly seen in our Scripture passage.

The first verse in our lesson marks a turning point in Jesus' ministry. The time of His death is approaching, and His disciples are not prepared for it. He keeps trying to get alone with them, but the multitudes constantly interrupt. The best He can do is instruct them as they travel from town to town (v. 27).

It seems appropriate, after leaving Galilee, to bring up the subject in the vicinity of the city Caesarea Philippi (established and named for Tiberius Caesar by Herod

Philip). Around this city there lay many villages or suburbs of historical significance. Not far away was snow-capped Mount Hermon. The worship of Baal once flourished nearby. According to legend the god of nature was born there. A marble temple named for Tiberius Caesar could be seen. The Jordan River flowed through this area—bringing back memories of Israel's defeats and deliverances. Yes, this place was appropriate because many voices from past and present were calling.

This was a place of *DECISION.*

"Whom Do Men Say That I Am?" (v. 27)

Jesus asked for two reasons: (1) As an *indirect* way of bringing up the matter of who He was and of His approaching death; (2) because a person's *beliefs*—assumptions and perspectives—in time come to determine one's actions. The multitudes had followed Jesus for numerous reasons (personal, physical, political, etc.). But unless their attitude toward Him is deep enough, they will cease to follow Him. Indeed, from this point on, as Jesus' demands became clearer, His followers became fewer.

The disciples reported the opinions of the people. Some thought He was another *John the Baptist,* preparing the way for the Messiah. Some thought this forerunner would be called Elijah, the one who settles disputes. (Many disputes were dismissed by the sentence: "They must wait the coming of Elijah.") Some thought He was a returned prophet (Jeremiah, says Matthew), or another in the line of prophets.

Jesus was disappointed with these answers. He had portrayed himself as a combination of the "Son of Man" and the "suffering servant." It was clear the populace considered Him only in light of their selfish hopes and dreams. They did not acknowledge Him as *unique.*

Thus Jesus narrowed the circumference of His questioning: *"Whom Say Ye That I Am?"*

Again, Jesus asked for two reasons: (1) He looked for personal comfort and understanding of His mission— surely He could expect this from those who knew Him best. (2) In the nature of the case, the question requires a *personal* answer. The opinion of others is important, but not most important. Personal decision is inescapable.

The disciples had discussed this before. For example, when Jesus calmed the sea, they asked: "What manner of man is this?" (Matt. 8:27; Mark 4:41; Luke 8:25). But deliberation can't go on forever. Decision must be made.

Peter expressed their corporate decision: "Thou art the Christ" (v. 29). But confession was not made in full awareness of the implications. To the disciples "Christ" simply meant "Messiah," "Anointed One"—a king, a throne on earth. With Him the disciples would reign. The confession was genuine but unaware. Thus Jesus directed them to "tell no man" (v. 30).

Awareness, or lack of it, inevitably affects our commitment.

"And He (Jesus) Began to Teach Them" (v. 31)

That is, now He began to do so *plainly.* He had taught the disciples before, but they had not taken good notes. In His opening ministry He said: "Destroy this temple, and in three days I will raise it up" (John 2:19). His words to Nicodemus are instructive: "As Moses lifted up the serpent in the wilderness, even so must the Son of man be lifted up" (3:14). To the Pharisees who sought a sign He said: "As

Jonas was three days and three nights in the whale's belly; so shall the Son of man be three days and three nights in the heart of the earth" (Matt. 12:40). When He fed the 5,000, He taught them: "I am the living bread which came down from heaven: if any man eat of this bread, he shall live for ever: and the bread that I will give is my flesh, which I will give for the life of the world" (John 6:51). In His shepherd sermon, He said: "I am the good shepherd: the good shepherd giveth his life for the sheep. . . . As the Father knoweth me, even so know I the Father: and I lay down my life for the sheep" (John 10:11, 15).

Yes, Jesus had taught them before. But He had to deal with them like a teacher does with the immature student. He had given the lectures; now He had to tell them what would be on the exam—they couldn't discern for themselves.

And like the immature student, they thought the exam too hard, and complained. There is usually one in the class who expresses the sentiment of the entire group. Predictably, Peter registered the complaint (v. 32).

But like a wise teacher, Jesus did not eliminate nor soften the exam. The student must not dictate to the teacher. "Get thee behind me, Satan," Jesus responded. Man cannot dictate to God. "Peter, you are thinking Satan's thoughts, not God's."

And thus *Jesus taught them of His coming agony and death* (v. 31), and He continued to do so in the days that followed, as in Matthew's Gospel. In His parable of the wicked husbandmen, the husbandmen said: "This is the heir [son]; come, let us *kill* him, and let us seize on his inheritance" (21:38). In Galilee He said: "The Son of Man shall be betrayed into the hands of men: and they shall *kill* him, and the third day he shall be raised again" (17:22-23). And on the way to Jerusalem: "The Son of man shall be betrayed unto the chief priests and unto the scribes, and they shall condemn him to death, and shall deliver him to the Gentiles to mock, and to scourge, and to *crucify* him: and the third day he shall rise again" (20:18-19, all italics added).

On this note of suffering the class session ended, evidently interrupted by the crowd (v. 34).

"And When He Had Called the People . . ." (v. 34)

The time had come to break the news to the crowds. Any who would be Jesus' disciple must fully accept the demands (vv. 34-38). Those who would continue to follow the Master must carry "his" cross.

APPLICATION TO CHRISTIANS APPROACHING THE 21st CENTURY

The heart of Mark's Gospel and of the entire New Testament is encapsulated in this momentous passage of Scripture. The stages of the Christian journey and the demands of commitment are powerfully obvious. They include four points: *decision, death, discipleship, destiny.*

I. DECISION (vv. 27-30)

The initial step in becoming a Christian is to decide for Christ, to confess "Jesus is Lord." This is not a mere mental assent to a creed. It is a commitment of the will, a complete trust of the total self—for "no man can say that Jesus is the Lord, but by the Holy [Spirit]" (1 Cor. 12:3). To decide for Christ is to become a "new creature" *in Christ Jesus* through repentance and faith.

95

But the beginning Christian cannot possibly comprehend all that is involved in this confession. The confession is genuine but inadequate. At significant points in the Christian life, after the initial decision, there is a battle with one's selfish ego. One wants to serve God, but in the way one wants to do it. This stage of the Christian life, after the initial ecstasy of conversion, can be miserable. Inner struggle and ambivalence of will are dominant. This "unfriendliness" to God's total will can mar one's peace, obscure spiritual vision, interrupt communion with God, and cripple one's efforts to do good.

II. DEATH (vv. 31-34)

As the Christian grows and matures and progresses in obedience, he is slowly taught by the Holy Spirit the fuller implications of his confession. He sees there must be a death to the carnal, selfish self. Self-seeking, self-defense, and self-assertion must be rejected. In order truly to say yes to Christ, one must consciously say no to all selfish interest.

This death to self includes *self-denial* (v. 34). What is meant is not merely denying some *thing* to oneself—like not buying a new car until next year. It is deliberately and in full awareness of the cost to renounce *oneself*—to begin to live for God and others. Paul states it clearly: "That they which live should not henceforth live unto themselves, but unto him which died for them, and rose again" (2 Cor. 5:15). The meaning is captured in the apostle's testimony: "I am crucified with Christ." Literally, "With Christ I have been crucified and still remain dead; and no longer is it the ego that lives, but Christ is living in me" (Gal. 2:20).

Jesus describes this death as *"taking up the cross,"* that is, putting oneself in the position of a condemned man on his way to execution. In the Roman world the criminal almost always carried his own cross to the place of execution. Thus to take up the cross does not mean to suffer some irritation, or annoyance, or frustration. It means to go to the place of death.

The words *"deny"* and *"take up"* are in a specific tense, suggesting a specific point in time, an identifiable moment of Christian experience. There must come a moment in which the believer *dies* to his own selfish will. We describe this point of Christian experience as the definite crisis of entire sanctification. It is God's gift of grace wrought in the heart of the believer in response to consecration and faith.

III. DISCIPLESHIP (8:34b—9:1)

The second stage of the Christian's life is not the terminal one. One now is more completely suited for faster and greater growth and development, and for faithful and consistent discipleship. According to Jesus, one must continuously *"lose"* his life, and *"follow"* Jesus. *Follow* is in the continuous present tense. The meaning is, "Keep on following."

Life has meaning only as we lose it for God and others. One does not lose his voice by using it. Rather, by using it properly, one develops it. In giving ourselves, we save ourselves.

Jesus is reminding us that material things are nothing. If we give our best selves to gain them, what can we use to regain our souls? We will have nothing left with

97

which to bargain. As Jim Elliot put it, "He is no fool who gives what he cannot keep to gain what he cannot lose."[1]

True discipleship is both *unselfish* and *unashamed* (v. 38).

IV. DESTINY (9:2-8)

To Jesus' audience, He said, There are some standing here "which shall not taste of death, till they have seen the kingdom of God come with power." This was literally fulfilled in His transfiguration, which was witnessed by several of the disciples. The transfiguration of Jesus symbolizes the final glorification of all believers who at the last day shall have a body fashioned after the body of our resurrected Christ. This is the Christian's destiny. What is experienced now in the way of forgiveness (decision), cleansing (death), and fulfillment in service (discipleship) is only the first installment, the down payment of our final inheritance. And if the "earnest" is "joy unspeakable" (1 Pet. 1:8), what will our ultimate inheritance be!

But this destiny can come only after the earlier stages of confession and commitment.

CONCLUSION

What kind of Christian confession is ours? It may be genuine; but is it also unaware of the implications? Or is it fully aware of the commanded "death to self," and yet totally submissive? Only Pentecost can make us fully aware, entirely sanctified (cleansed and empowered), and prepared for discipleship. But Pentecost must be preceded by Calvary.

"Whosoever will come after me,
let him deny himself, and take up his cross,
and follow me" (v. 34).

RAYMOND W. HURN

General Superintendent

Raymond W. Hurn, born in Ontario, Oreg., is a graduate of Bethany Nazarene College. As a part of his ministry he served as a pastor (16 years) and as a district superintendent (9 years) in the Church of the Nazarene. During these years he was an active church starter.

He was elected executive secretary of the Department of Home Missions in 1968 and remained in this position for 17 years. He administered overseas home missions in Europe, Africa, and the South Pacific until 1976. Throughout his tenure he was very active in developing ethnic work and in stimulating local churches to start new works among ethnic groups. In recent years he spearheaded a new thrust in church planting throughout the denomination, resulting in 1,560 new fully organized churches from 1980 to 1985. He has been a leader in the American church growth movement, which brought the denomination into the forefront of this activity. He was a member of the 1974 Lausanne Congress on World Evangelization and serves on advisory and planning committees for Lausanne 1989. He served on advisory and program committees for Houston '85, a consultation on evangelizing ethnic America involving 40 denominations.

In conjunction with his home mission work he has authored several books and pamphlets to educate and prepare church members for the process of church growth and church planting. One of these, *Mission Possible*, became the first denomination-wide training text on home missions.

Dr. Hurn was elected as the 26th general superintendent in June 1985, during the General Assembly in Anaheim, Calif., after having moved to Colorado to teach in the Nazarene Bible College and consult in the church growth field.

He is married to the former Madelyn Kirkpatrick. The Hurns have two daughters, Jacque Oliver and Constance Isbell, and three grandchildren.

100

JOY IN THE FAMILY

SCRIPTURE: 1 John 1:4; 3

TEXT: "These things write we unto you that your joy may be full" (1:4).

First John, often called the "family Epistle," was written by John, the only one of the apostles to live to old age. His writings come at the end of his long career. In the late 80s or early 90s he wrote the Gospel of John. After that he wrote First John, Second John, Third John, and by A.D. 95 finished his writing contribution with the Revelation. He wrote against the heresies of gnosticism that were creeping into the church to destroy it. He wrote to instruct the family of God in how to be a friend of God.

John the apostle wrote like an apostle. His statements are pointed and authoritative, especially as he exposed error. He wrote in a commanding style befitting an apostle of great seniority. Though old, he is still one of the sons of thunder, referring to the heretics as being "antichrist" (2:18) and children of the devil (3:10).

John also wrote as an eyewitness to the events that shaped the life, ministry, death, and resurrection of Christ and those events that followed Pentecost. Matthew, Mark, and Luke talked about the miracles of Jesus and recorded His teachings. John interpreted the teachings and miracles of Jesus. His Gospel becomes the most theological of any of the Gospels because of his emphasis upon Christian belief. The main thrust of this family Epistle of John was joy for those who were members of the family of God.

Reconciliation, consciousness of sonship, growth in holiness, future glory all are but pieces of the picture embraced in John's view of eternal life that he saw as the authentic possession of those who experienced Christ's joy. This is not a new theme for the apostle John. In John 3 when he recorded the witness of John the Baptist he spoke of the joy that is fulfilled. The theme of John 15 centers in the word of Christ that "my joy might remain in you, and that your joy might be full" (v. 11).

I. *There Is a Uniqueness About John as a Conveyor of the Biblical Message*

When the moment had come for Christ to call out His first disciples, He went to the seashore and called first Simon Peter and Andrew, who were casting nets into the sea. And immediately after He went to James and John, sons of Zebedee, who were with their father in a ship mending nets. And when He called out to them, "they immediately left the ship and their father, and followed him" (Matt. 4:22). Their mother, Salome, became a very active follower of Christ also.

John had earned "the right" to speak to the Church in these final years of his life. He is the only apostle left, and his years are numbered. First John is an expression of the essence of a devout life sacrificially lived and is a distillation of his entire life and ministry. It is not surprising then that he would speak with intense passion and in intimate detail about the plan of God.

102

In the introduction to this Epistle he comes to the point immediately and personifies his concerns for the "Word of life." He testified that "we have seen" and "heard" Him, "touched" Him, and so, we "testify" to Him and "proclaim" Him to you. "The eternal life, which was with the Father . . . has appeared to us . . . so that you also may have fellowship with us. And our fellowship is with the Father and with his Son, Jesus Christ. We write this to make our joy complete" (1 John 1:1-4, NIV).

First John is sometimes referred to as the holy of holies of Scripture (the sanctum sanctorum). The holy of holies in the Old Testament was the place where the ark stood, and no one was permitted to enter into the holy of holies but the high priest, who could only enter once a year. The Book of First John occupies a similar position because of its spiritual insight, depth, and quality. John Wesley found 10 of his 30 favorite texts on perfect love hidden away in this small Book of First John. John wrote with intensity because of the historicity of the occasion. He had been so much a part of all of the ministry of Christ and of the apostles. There is an intimacy about the writing of John.

John wrote to draw a line between the world of evil and the true Church of the living God. He came with a message of simplicity, which he gave in a direct style of presentation. John's message divides easily into a walk to be pursued, cleansing for each child of God to experience, and a fellowship to be enjoyed.

II. *A Walk to Be Pursued*

"But if we walk in the light, as he is in the light, we have fellowship with one another, and the blood of Jesus, his Son, purifies us from all sin" (1 John 1:7, NIV).

The Christian is to walk in the light of God, who is the essence of light and in whom there is no darkness. Light was often associated with the Divine Being in Scripture.

The Psalmist declared of God, "You are very great; you are clothed with splendor and majesty. He wraps himself in light as with a garment; he stretches out the heavens like a tent" (104:1-2, NIV). To Daniel, God revealed deep and hidden things and knew "what lies in darkness, and light dwells with him" (2:22, NIV). To James God was "the Father of lights," in whom was no variableness nor shadow of turning (1:17). Peter announced that it was God "who hath called you out of darkness into his marvellous light" (1 Pet. 2:9).

Paul exhorted the Ephesian Christians, "Once you were darkness, but now you are light in the Lord; walk as children of light" (5:8, RSV). John in his Gospel declared that Christ was "the light of the world" (8:12; 9:5), and that His "life was the light of men" (1:4). The light itself cannot create spiritual life, but it does quicken and develop and strengthen so that life can be created as men walk in the light of God. To "walk" is an expression frequently used in Scripture indicating the entire life being lived. When John urged that the family of God not "walk in darkness" but walk in the light, he underscored a basic principle leading to joy in the family of God. God who is the essence of light causes the darkness to flee away. The holiness of God fits the symbolism of light, and it is the glory of His being. John declared, "In him is no darkness at all." It is the light of God that will dispel darkness.

One of the great concerns of John was the heresy of the Gnostics. These people who professed to devote themselves to the pursuit of the highest and holiest knowledge were guilty of the vilest sins with their bodies. Their profession was characterized as being the practice of a lie. Since the body was considered evil by the Gnostics, it was to be treated harshly. And so asceticism grew (see Col. 2:21—3:5). This dualism also led to licentiousness. The reasoning was that since matter and not the breaking of God's law was considered evil, breaking His law was of no moral consequence. Later this gnosticism of the early era would be intricately developed into a complex moral system. John proposed that we must "walk in the light." This is an expression frequently used in Scripture indicating the entire life. To walk in darkness is to live in the practice of sin.

"If we say that we have fellowship with him, and walk in darkness, we lie" (1:6). John warned against a practice that was opposed to the truth of God. While John warned against this unbiblical dualism that flowed from the heretical errors, he was not successful in destroying gnosticism in his day. It flowered and flourished long after John was gone. It may remain today, in modern form, as a danger to the Church.

Holiness is the one single word that best describes the meaning of the apostle's phrase, "walking in the light." It is living a life that is in sympathy with holiness. But more than that, it is a walk that creates within us a heart that beats in total harmony with the light of God. The life becomes the practice of holiness. Inward principles and beliefs are expressed in outward behavior. The one who is walking in the light is progressing in holiness, not stationary but advancing.

105

III. *As We Walk in the Light There Is a Cleansing to Be Experienced*

As a consequence of walking in the light, John promised "the blood of Jesus Christ his Son cleanseth us from all sin." Those who walk in the light will feel their need of this cleansing. We are required to walk in all the light of God if we do indeed experience the cleansing. The beginning journey of walking in the light may bring to the surface those sinful practices out of harmony with God. But as sinful darkness is exposed to the candlepower of God's light, a cleansing will take place.

John emphasized that the blood of Jesus denotes the sacrifice of the life of Jesus for our cleansing. The power of the sacrifice lies in the power of a pure and holy love. This is a mighty expression of God's love toward us. For He "spared not his own Son, but delivered him up for us all . . . who gave himself for us, that he might redeem us from all iniquity, and purify unto himself a people for his own possession, zealous of good works" (Rom. 8:32; Titus 2:14, ASV).

The apostle John used the present tense. He did not use the past tense, "cleansed." He spoke of the cleansing in the now. The thoroughness of the moral cleansing that takes place in the human heart is emphasized when John said, "He cleanseth us from all sin." There is no sin so devastating, so hurtful, so deeply embedded that it cannot be cleansed from the human heart.

There are those who may deny that there is any personal sin. John answers in verse 8, "If we say that we have no sin, we deceive ourselves, and the truth is not in us." Often many deny the blessing by affirming that they are free from sin when actual sin does remain. Some claim good deeds that should buy them merit, offsetting sinfulness. The Pharisees claimed many generous and kind deeds. When we compare ourselves with the work of others whom we deem to be inferior, it is easy to conclude that we have no sin. The denial of sin often comes when we do not understand what the Bible really teaches about sin.

Again, the promise of John is steadfast. "If we confess our sins, he is faithful and just to forgive us our sins, and to cleanse us from all unrighteousness. If we say that we have not sinned, we make him a liar, and his word is not in us" (vv. 9-10).

An open confession of need for the cleansing baptism of the Holy Spirit and a sincere seeking after this cleansing will bring results.

IV. *There Is a Fellowship to Be Experienced as We Walk in the Light*

John's mighty prayer was that our "joy may be full," that we may be fulfilled in our experience and our relationship with Jesus Christ. John had only one ambition for the Church, and that was that they may have the joy of the Lord fulfilled in themselves, resulting in a fellowship that goes beyond human ties, human admiration, and human respect. This fellowship experienced with Christ and His people is unique, uplifting, and glorious.

There is fellowship with all of the saints of God and with Christ, our Savior—"fellowship one with another." As we walk in the atmosphere of truthfulness, true righteousness, and love, we are drawn into fellowship with those who also walk in truth, righteousness, and love. There is a sharing of goals, of purposes, of aspirations.

There is a growing together in unity, in character, in service, in ultimate objectives. The communion established is something that is genuine and blessed. It is called "fellowship with the saints." Our fellowship is also with our Heavenly Father. The spirit of oneness with Him and fellowship with Him makes the more sweet our fellowship with the people of God, as described in chapter 3 of this Epistle:

"Beloved, now are we the sons of God, and it doth not yet appear what we shall be: but we know that, when he shall appear, we shall be like him; for we shall see him as he is. And every man that hath this hope in him purifieth himself, even as he is pure" (vv. 2-3).

"The Son of God was manifested, that he might destroy the works of the devil. Whosoever is born of God doth not commit sin; for his seed remaineth in him: and he cannot sin, because he is born of God" (vv. 8-9).

"We know that we have passed from death unto life, because we love the brethren. He that loveth not his brother abideth in death. . . . Hereby perceive we the love of God, because he laid down his life for us: and we ought to lay down our lives for the brethren" (vv. 14, 16).

"And this is his commandment, That we should believe on the name of his Son Jesus Christ, and love one another, as he gave us commandment. . . . And hereby we know that he abideth in us, by the Spirit which he hath given us" (vv. 23-24).

Does your heart hunger for this fellowship? It is a result of walking in the light until His Spirit cleanses from all sin.

THE RIVER OF BLESSING

SCRIPTURE: John 7:37-39

TEXT: *"On the last and greatest day of the Feast, Jesus stood and said in a loud voice, 'If anyone is thirsty, let him come to me and drink. Whoever believes in me, as the Scripture has said, streams of living water will flow from within him.' By this he meant the Spirit, whom those who believed in him were later to receive"* (NIV).*

In the Word of God there are many symbols for the Holy Spirit. Sometimes He is referred to as refiner's fire or the oil of joy. On the Day of Pentecost the Holy Spirit was described as being something like a "rushing mighty wind" (Acts 2:2, KJV). Here in John 7 we find the record of Christ expressing himself to a maximum audience on an important feast day. He even interrupted the proceedings to declare that if anyone was "thirsty," he could come and drink, and the work of the Holy Spirit would be as "streams of living water" flowing from within.

John 7 contains many references to the opposers who hated Christ. The descriptions are pointed. "The Jews . . . were waiting to take his life" (v. 1). "The Jews

---

*Unless otherwise indicated, all Scripture quotations are from *The Holy Bible, New International Version.*

109

were watching for him and asking, 'Where is that man?'" (v. 11). "Others replied, '. . . he deceives the people.' But no one would say anything publicly about him for fear of the Jews" (vv. 12-13). Jesus asked them, "Why are you trying to kill me?" (v. 19). The people of Jerusalem began to ask, "Isn't this the man they are trying to kill?" (v. 25). "At this they tried to seize him, but no one laid a hand on him" (v. 30). "Then the chief priests and the Pharisees sent temple guards to arrest him" (v. 32). "The people were divided because of Jesus. Some wanted to seize him, but no one laid a hand on him" (vv. 43-44).

Out of this background and atmosphere of hatred and evil intent we find Christ declaring one of the most important truths of New Testament teaching. It is a declaration that there is an experience that overcomes selfishness, greed, and carnality and becomes a stream of personal spiritual refreshment. It is a declaration that out of the sanctified life a stream of blessing will flow to the Church in unexpected ways. It is an implication that this river is a stream of life-giving power to the world.

What a message! And what a setting in which to state one of the most important truths of all the ages.

I. *Jesus Chose a Significant Occasion in Which to Present the Scriptural Truth of Rivers of Living Water*

It was the time for the Feast of the Tabernacles. This was one of three major annual feasts observed by the Jews: the Feast of the Passover, the Feast of Pentecost, and the Feast of Tabernacles.

The Feast of Tabernacles was held between September and October and lasted for seven days. They lived in tents, arbors, or other temporary places. All of the Jewish males were required to attend. This feast was commanded in Exod. 23:16; 34:22; Lev. 23:39, 42-43. It was a harvest home festival, a feast of ingathering, and commemorated the dwelling of Israel in tents in the wilderness. It was sometimes called the Feast of Booths.

The purpose of this feast was to remind the people in their prosperity of the days of their homelessness, that they might not forget God, who had delivered them from bondage.

The modern-day camp meeting could be thought of as a counterpart to this Old Testament Feast of Tabernacles. Whether we do it in the midst of an enormous crowd in a packed camp meeting tabernacle or whether we do it in a small group in a small place, it is good for us to have seasons of remembering God's mercy and grace. We need to remember those days without God's presence in contrast to the reality of His present goodness, mercy, and blessing bestowed upon us today.

Since everybody was required to attend the Feast of Tabernacles, the brothers of Jesus were a bit exercised with Him because He implied that He would not go up with them to the Feast of Tabernacles. They said to Him, "'No one who wants to become a public figure acts in secret. Since you are doing these things, show yourself to the world.' For even his own brothers did not believe in him" (7:4-5).

Jesus replied that the right time had not yet come.

About the middle of the feast Jesus did go up to the Feast of Tabernacles in secret. By this time the Jews who were watching for Him were whispering among themselves, "Where is *that* man?" And the crowds were joining in the whispering, which was very widespread. Only the crowds were saying something different from the Jewish leaders. They were saying, "He is a good man." But some were saying, "He deceives the people." The whispering continued privately with nothing being said in public because they feared the Jewish leaders. Midway in the feast Christ began teaching. The Jews marveled because He said, "My doctrine is not mine, but his that sent me. If any man do his will, he shall know of the doctrine, whether it be of God, or whether I speak of myself" (7:16-17, KJV).

Each of the seven mornings of the feast days the people had gone to the Fountain of Siloam where the priest filled the golden pitcher and brought it back to the Temple with music and joyful shouts. He emptied the golden pitcher of water toward the west when the people cried, "Lift up thy hand." Then toward the east he emptied a cup of wine and the people chanted the words, "With joy shall ye draw water out of the wells of salvation" (Isa. 12:3, KJV). This ceremony reminded the people of how Moses brought forth water from the rock. On the last day this particular ceremony was omitted. The last day was the eighth day, and a closing assembly was held. On this last day it was designated a great day of testimony and joy and was called the Day of Great Hosanna.

It was on this last day when their minds were so filled with thoughts of the final ceremony of Great Hosanna that Jesus saw the multitudes with their weariness and thirstiness of soul, making long pilgrimages through the generations but thirsting and fainting in spirit. Although Jewish leaders usually sat when they taught, it was on this last day that Jesus stood, drawing attention to himself and to the message. And in this last day, the great day of the feast, He stood and cried, "'If anyone is thirsty, let him come to me and drink. Whoever believes in me, . . . streams of living water will flow from within him.' By this he meant the Spirit . . . Up to that time the Spirit had not been given, since Jesus had not yet been glorified" (7:37-39).

II. *The "Rivers of Living Waters" from John 7 Is Not to Be Confused with the "Wells of Springing Water" in the Message of Jesus from John 4:13*

In John 4 we find the record of Christ and His evangelistic party stopping near a well in Samaria. While the disciples purchased food in the nearby town, Jesus carried on a conversation with a Samaritan woman. He told her that everyone who drank from that well would be thirsty again. But whoever, He said, "drinks the water I give him will never thirst. Indeed, the water I give him will become in him a spring of water welling up to eternal life" (John 4:14).

The woman longed for this water that would keep her from getting thirsty. Jesus asked her to call her husband. And she responded, "I have no husband." Jesus said, "You are right" because you "have had five husbands, and the man you now have is not your husband" (John 4:17-18).

This encounter with the Samaritan woman is one of the most beautiful portraits of Christ. She returned to the city and led a multitude of Samaritans back to the feet of Jesus. So many were touched by the divine Spirit of God that they pled for Him to stay with them, and He did remain two extra days to explain to them this well of water springing up into everlasting life. Undoubtedly, this was one of the greatest evangelistic ingatherings in the ministry of Jesus. He reached across the cultural barriers of race and tribe to win these Gentiles.

He refused food when the disciples returned, saying, "My food . . . is to do the will of him who sent me." They had a saying among themselves that it is four months until harvest. He admonished them, "Open your eyes and look at the fields! They are ripe for harvest" (4:34-35). They had not had any conversation about sowing seed or harvesting crops. Jesus simply saw in the spiritual hunger of a woman and that of a town's people a ripened harvest field. Many drank from the fountain of living water and became new creatures in Christ Jesus.

What Jesus taught in John 7 concerned those who were already believers. He said, "He that believeth on me" (v. 38, KJV), referrring to the Spirit believers were later to receive. Undoubtedly it is a reference to the approaching Pentecost. This teaching does not imply that the Spirit did not yet live in believers. It does imply that the Spirit would come in a sanctifying work, as a second experience in the believer's heart when personal Pentecost was experienced.

III. *What Is the Practical Meaning of This Symbol of the Holy Spirit Being like "Rivers of Living Water"?*

In the King James Version the promise of verse 38 is "out of his belly shall flow rivers of living water." The *New International Version* translates these words, "streams of living water will flow from within him."

Recently I came down with a slight calcification of a tendon—generally referred to as tendonitis. To relieve the

114

pain and inflammation the doctor gave medication that had a reverse effect so the ankles continued to swell even when the pain and inflammation had apparently disappeared. But before they could come to a final conclusion they did many tests with special attention to the blood, at one point testing the supply of blood that ran through the arteries down to the toes and returning through the veins—a venous test that showed "all clear." It reminded me that a "river" of blood flows out of the belly, pumped by the heart through the arteries and back through minute channels in the veins. The system works well unless something happens to plug arteries or veins.

Jesus often used physical symbols to reveal a spiritual truth, as He has done in this passage. The sinful person, like the woman at the Samaritan well thirsting for spiritual life, can drink of the living water and be made a new creature in Christ Jesus (John 4). The believer thirsts for more of God, for heart cleansing, for removal of the "bent to sinning" (Charles Wesley) so prevalent in the carnal but believing heart (John 7).

The promise that Jesus made in John 7 was that the "hunger" or "thirst" for God can be satisfied. The believer's heart can be filled with spiritual power, and the sanctified life can be like rivers of living water. The symbolism is beautiful. Rivers do symbolize power to shed light, as they are often harnessed to make electricity. Rivers are harnessed to carry heavy burdens. The ships, barges, and boats carry the commerce of a nation.

There is a difference in the walk, witness, and work of the Christian after having been empowered by the Holy Spirit. This experience forms outlets of service in the sanctified life, improving and making more joyous the personal walk with God.

This river becomes a stream of personal, spiritual refreshment to the born-again, sanctified child of God. Originating deep in the nature of man, it becomes an uninhibited flow, unhindered by selfishness, greed, or carnality, and strengthened by full commitment to do the will of God.

This river is a stream of blessing to the church in unexpected ways. The more we commit ourselves to God and receive of His Spirit, the easier we are on other people in the church. In direct proportion to the numbers of people who experience the blessing of holiness and walk in the power of the Spirit, the tide of fellowship rises.

This river is a stream of life-giving power to the world. We must not hide our light under a bushel. We must not be shy to proclaim this witness. The sanctified life must be brought into contact with carnal personalities where by example, witness, and testimony we get beyond nominality in the church and become vibrant, soul-winning evangels to change the climate of our society.

In my sophomore year at Bethany Nazarene College (now SNU) under the preaching of I. C. Mathis, my eyes were opened to the need for a second experience that would go beyond what I had received in the Kingman, Kans., church. I was startled by the sense of conviction that I felt for heart cleansing and empowerment of the Holy Spirit. After all, I had professed to have that experience of heart holiness while a high school student.

I was so overcome with a sense of need and so baffled by this sense of need that I stayed in my room all day, cutting classes and reporting "sick" on my job. During my night and day of wrestling with God I found 1 John 1:7, which read, "If we walk in the light, as he is in the light, we have fellowship one with another, and the blood of Jesus Christ his Son cleanseth us from all sin" (KJV). I knew the instant that I read that verse that it described both my condition and my need and had the formula for complete release and fulfillment.

My problem was that the devil gave me a great sense of self-importance by reminding me that there were many who had confidence in me. I began to think about students who had sought the Lord under my preaching and some who had come to the school as students as a result of some of those revivals. It was almost too much for me to handle. I wrestled all night and all day and decided that I would walk in the light of God no matter what it cost me and no matter how it looked to my friends and to fellow students.

I was the first seeker that night at the altar, crying out to God for more of Him, for complete cleansing of inbred sin, and for the Holy Spirit to fill my life. Dr. L. T. Corlett sat down on the platform steps in front of me after a season of prayer and said, "Ray, in the Word of God we read, 'If we walk in the light, as he is in the light, we have fellowship one with another, and the blood of Jesus Christ his Son cleanseth us from all sin'" (1 John 1:7, KJV). I prayed again and with deep commitment reminded God that I was trying to "walk in all the light." And 1 John 1:7 was the promise that I claimed for my victory. Soon a student friend knelt beside me and put his arm around me and said, "Ray, 1 John tells us, 'If we walk in the light, as he is in the light, we have fellowship one with another, and the blood of Jesus Christ his Son cleanseth us from all sin.'"

That night I knew that my commitment was total, complete, without reservation. A sweet peace flooded my soul. I knew God had heard my prayer. There was a sense of fellowship and oneness with Him and with all of God's people that made me know that the work was done.

A strange and wonderful thing happened the next morning. After breakfast had been served, and eaten, we had family devotions. The young lady chosen to read the scripture said that she felt especially led that day to read the first chapter of John. My heart was so full that I could scarcely contain myself. When she read again the seventh verse of the first chapter of 1 John, waves of blessing, of affirmation, and of great joy flooded my soul to know that I was in complete oneness with God and in fellowship with Him. These events took place in the spring of 1941. In the nearly 50 years since that moment I have never knowingly or consciously taken one thing off the altar. I have kept my vows to God and have walked in the light through good times and bad times, through difficulties and great problems, through temptations and trials. And through these years I have had a great sense of fulfillment in being in the center of God's will. My greatest delight is to serve Him.

Notes

CHAPTER 2:

1. Oswald Chambers, *He Shall Glorify Me* (Fort Washington, Pa.: Christian Literature Crusade, 1965), 105.

2. Clovis G. Chappell, *Sermons from Job* (Nashville: Abingdon, 1957), 93.

3. John Wesley, "A Plain Account of Christian Perfection," *The Works of John Wesley,* 3rd ed. (reprint: Kansas City: Beacon Hill Press of Kansas City, 1978), 11:380.

4. *Works,* 6:509.

5. Alan Redpath, *Victorious Christian Service: Studies in the Book of Nehemiah* (Westwood, N.J.: Fleming H. Revell Co., 1958), 117-19.

6. Harold John Ockenga, *Power Through Pentecost* (Grand Rapids: William B. Eerdmans Publishing Co., 1959), 7-8, 14.

7. John T. Seamands, *On Tiptoe with Joy* (Kansas City: Beacon Hill Press of Kansas City, 1967), 64-67.

CHAPTER 4:

1. *Manual of the Church of the Nazarene* (Kansas City: Nazarene Publishing House, 1985), 25.

CHAPTER 5:

1. Ἁγιασον, from ʽα, *negative,* and γῆ, *the earth. The New Testament of Our Lord and Saviour Jesus Christ* (New York: Methodist Book Concern, n.d.), 1:639.

2. *The Interpreter's Bible* (New York and Nashville: Abingdon-Cokesbury Press, 1951), 7:266.

3. William M. Greathouse, *The Fullness of the Spirit* (Kansas City: Nazarene Publishing House, 1958), 61-62.

4. C. K. Barrett, *The Gospel According to Saint John* (London: Society for the Publication of Christian Knowledge, 1966),

427 (italics added). Also, William Temple, *Readings in St. John's Gospel* (New York: St. Martin's Press, 1968), 312.

    5. Nazarene *Manual,* par. 801, 223.

    6. Ibid., art. 10, par. 13, 28.

CHAPTER 6:

    1. "Plain Account," 11:394.

    2. "The Scripture Way of Salvation," *Works,* 6:46, 52.

    3. Greek τέλειος *(teleios).*

    4. *The Westminster Shorter Catechism,* Q. 1.

    5. "Plain Account," *Works,* 11:430.

    6. "The Doctrine of Original Sin," *Works,* 9:456.

    7. Based on Heb. 11:1 and Rom. 10:17. For Wesley, faith is not believing a proposition; it is an inward persuasion or conviction, produced by the Word and the Spirit, a divine assurance that God is faithful to perform what He has promised.

    8. 'ολοτελεῖς *(holoteleis).*

    9. "The Scripture Way," *Works,* 6:52-54.

CHAPTER 10:

    1. Elisabeth Elliot, *Shadow of the Almighty: The Life and Testament of Jim Elliot* (New York: Harpers and Bros., Publishers, 1958), 247.